IF Y⬤U WERE THERE

Francisco Garcia

IF YOU WERE THERE

MISSING PEOPLE AND THE MARKS THEY LEAVE BEHIND

MUDLARK

Mudlark
HarperCollins*Publishers*
1 London Bridge Street
London SE1 9GF

www.harpercollins.co.uk

HarperCollins*Publishers*
1st Floor, Watermarque Building, Ringsend Road
Dublin 4, Ireland

First published by Mudlark 2021

3 5 7 9 10 8 6 4 2

A catalogue record of this book is
available from the British Library

ISBN 978-0-00-841215-9

Printed and bound in Great Britain by
CPI Group (UK) Ltd, Croydon

MIX
Paper from
responsible sources
FSC™ C007454

This book is produced from independently certified FSC™ paper
to ensure responsible forest management.

For more information visit: www.harpercollins.co.uk/green

To my wonderful family

I sometimes wonder what was disappeared first – among all the things that have vanished from the island.

The Memory Police by Yoko Ogawa

CONTENTS

PART I
STEPHANIE AND CHRISTOBAL

CHAPTER 1

Of all the everyday, occasionally comforting lies we tell ourselves and others, the idea of a 'first memory' is perhaps one of the most powerful. It's a nice enough thought. The first intrusions of consciousness and colour, the very first indications of being here, beyond the sensory oblivion of earliest childhood. I tend to find that the people I ask for theirs only want to admit to the resolutely banal and believable, though perhaps that is just the truth of the matter. First memories are such a uniquely personal, fractured thing. And just like our dreams, they lose so much of their individual power when dissected out loud and at the mercy of another person's capacity for boredom. As I get older, I find myself more and more intrigued by what people are liable to recall. For some, those first flashes seem to prove something significant; perhaps even a portent of the life they've happened to live since. For others, they mean nothing at all outside of the accidents of memory.

I'm still not quite sure where I sit between these two poles. It's not that my first recollections are anything remotely special, far from it. If I close my eyes and cast back there's the usual jumble, smoothed into neatness by many years of practice. And there I am, suddenly aware of earth and summer heat, sitting by the small cluster of trees at the end of a small concrete garden. Above me there is greenery mixed with sunlight and a few lengthening shadows. To my left, the shape of a door pointing to a shaded, tiled kitchen itself leading back into what I now understand as signifying home then, the shoddily converted bottom half of a crumbling Victorian house in Hither Green, in the seemingly endless and exasperated depths of south-east London. In place of any definite sound, there is an atmosphere, at once heavy and content, the unmistakable indolence of an afternoon in high summer. And there is the feeling of something, someone, else. A larger figure, tucked halfway out of sight, watching unobtrusively. Their presence is part of the scene's security. It's the shape of a slightly stooped young man, rake thin and verging on the edge of frailty. It is the outline of my father, Christobal Garcia-Ferrera, as he watches on from his vantage point on a plastic garden chair, content enough to let me roam, as long as I remain in his line of vision.

There's no way of saying with total precision when this fleeting domestic scene played out, but some rudimentary detective work tells me it must be around 1995. I was born three years earlier, less than a mile up the road at Lewisham Hospital, with the certificate signed by both Christobal and my mother, Stephanie Garcia-Ferrera. I arrived on the late afternoon of 13 July 1992. A newly born responsibility, to be tended to and doted on. Naturally, Mum had it hardest that day. I'd had to be cut from her, a caesarean delivery at the end of a relatively uncomplicated pregnancy spent mainly in the cocoon of the local area. The afternoon was backdropped by heavy rainfall, just one predictable hazard of any London summer. And yes, he was present – though not the whole way through. He could be excitable like that, it was just in his nature, the need to fidget and pace like a slightly unruly child.

My gran – my mother's mother – used to tell me the story with a still disbelieving chuckle, many years later. Christobal (Chris, as he'd always been known here) couldn't quite stick with the protracted drama of the labour hours and had headed out into the car park and the nearby streets to pace and pirouette, a ball of anguish and coiled up excitement. But when the all-clear came, how he rushed back in to be by Mum's side and take me up in his arms. For some never quite explained reason, it was my hands he was most taken with, at least that's how Gran told it. 'My son,' he was said to have shouted, grabbing any nurse and passer-by who would listen, 'has the most incredible hands!' Gran always did love to tell that story, needing only the very slightest excuse to prompt a full recital. Were it possible, I'd like to tease Christobal about its veracity and that of all the other little narrative flourishes that day has since been wrapped in. But that has not been possible, for many years now.

They had first met in Spain. At the very southern tip of Andalusia, where Europe dissolves into Morocco and the rest of North Africa. In La Línea de la Concepción, a small and perpetually troubled coastal city of fewer than 70,000 people, not far from the geographic and territorial oddity of Gibraltar. Christobal's hometown and almost all he knew before his new life in London. For as long as anyone can remember, it had been a city of smugglers and bandits; a frontier town founded as a bulwark against English conquest and only given formal recognition by the Spanish state in the late nineteenth century. What can I say about his family there other than the fragments that I've come to know, over the years. A sprawling, working-class clan, with many siblings and cousins, most of whom lived and worked in the city or its periphery. Perhaps that's one of the things that appealed to Mum, on their first meetings. She was a Londoner, whose adulthood had grown to be marked by an increasingly intense love affair with all things Iberian. It had stemmed from a trip to Granada with her eldest sister, some years before, in the late 1980s. There's a photo that still lives in my aunt's house from that first trip. Mum, sitting in the window of a cloister, sheltered from the dazzling afternoon light outside. With one hand resting under her chin, her eyes pointed out to an invisible horizon, a scene of almost religious contemplation and tranquillity, like something from a Rossetti print.

From that first visit, it's said that she knew the country to be more like home than anything she'd known before. It had something to do with the vibrancy of colour, the subtle grades of light. These weren't things you found too often in Catford or Forest Hill, or whichever part of London she found herself living in during those long years before. But it usually takes more than just a different quality of light to fall properly in love. Mum was a middle child and a quiet, sometimes painfully shy young woman, having struggled with eating disorders and self-confidence in her peripatetic teenage years dotting between London council flats with Gran and her youngest sister. Perhaps as a consequence, she possessed a well-developed gift for secrecy, her life subdivided into tight self-contained compartments, sometimes kept hidden from even the family and friends she was closest to. Yet there were also the passions that she couldn't help but wear on her sleeve. Poetry and travel, mythology and the idiosyncratic patterns of Romani history. For many years she had herself lived with one leg in a local traveller community, growing her light-brown hair past her waist and immersing herself in their ways of life. There is talk of another man from that time, though few, if any, from our family ever had the chance to meet him and, in truth, no one now can even quite be sure of his name. He was just another silent part of her life. The same aunt who first took her to Spain once described her to me as having an invisible layer of skin missing; as a young girl she would often burn the poetry and stories she had written, the shame of them being seen by any other living eye being something too much to bear.

This is not to say Mum lacked resilience. You don't tend to leave alone for a foreign country as a woman in your early thirties without it, which is precisely what she managed after saving for a few months from her job as an admin assistant at Lambeth Council, from right after that first holiday. And an hour of Spanish every night, like clockwork, in preparation to realise the dream of a new existence. She made it real, soon enough after. It's here that the timeline falters slightly, at least in my telling of it. It must have been in the last years of the eighties when they met. Christobal was considerably younger than Mum, almost by a decade. Perhaps she was his first serious love and catalyst to a kind of adulthood he'd barely known to be possible. He was young, but his looks were never exactly boyish. Heavy browed, with serious features, you could say he almost looked older than his years, despite his slight frame and height, at little over five foot seven. And perhaps she fell in love with the strength of his enthusiasms, of which there were many. Flamenco music and dance, as well as the Spanish guitar and amateur boxing. Then, of course, there was his capacity for a good time and late nights, a specially refined talent for carefree joy and spontaneity. No one has ever disputed the happiness of those first few months in Spain, right back at the root of their beginnings as a couple. As they passed, someone must have made a decision: it was time to return to London, only this time together, as a unit and, soon enough, as man and wife. I suppose I could spend many words trying to analyse their motives from my seat here, as a 27-year-old man, writing in my flat in one of those same drab south London neighbourhoods, but it wouldn't really do either of them justice. For him, there was the same promise of adventure and opportunity that his new wife must have felt coming to Spain for the first time. For her, the security of family and a stable enough income. For them both, the idea of perhaps trying for something they both wanted even more than each other: a child.

Here we arrive, on more solid ground. Where the facts start to become clearer and the narrative more precisely traced. It is here that I can almost begin to rely on official documents and the memories of others as a source, however unreliable they might occasionally be. The new start in London did not herald the beginning of a gilded fairy tale, not that either of them had really expected it would. They arrived back to precisely what she'd left behind – a London both greyscale and chaotic, at the fag end of the Thatcher years. Whatever kind of giddily nauseous boom had been birthed by the deregulatory 'Big Bang' in the financial hubs of the old City had not blown south into her orbit. Life moved along steady lines, built around the hubs of home, work and a steady network of family, friends and neighbours. South London really was different then, a slightly ragged outpost set against the arrogance and noise of the city proper. When the streets felt that bit wider and the distance to escape that bit longer. The land of the rock-solid nowherevilles of Lewisham High Street and Rushey Green.

It could be magical, if you knew an inroad to its hidden charms, as she did. There were some good times in store for Mum and Christobal in those first few years in the city. Life still had that last slight tinge of weightlessness, of relative freedom and at least most of the opportunities that the circumstances of their class and lack of money permitted. Many weekends were spent whittling away the nights in drink and raucous song; Christobal, Mum, my aunt and her close friends, in whoever's flat seemed to be the best fit for the evening in hand. Sometimes they would be joined by a few of his relatives from back home, including his favourite cousin, Marie Pelle, who would provide accompaniment on the guitar.

But enjoying the nights had never been his problem. Soon it was clear that the days brought other things, the first onset of trouble and failure. Christobal's English was always ok, if occasionally broken. It was fine when Mum was there to translate and smooth over any difficulties and anyway, most people were understanding enough of a young man trying to give his best. But his best was not always enough, poised against the obstinacy or spite of others. He worked as a painter and decorator, a willing pair of hands in the unregulated world of odd jobs and off-the-books construction projects, a world wrapped in its own tightly knit machismo and networks of favouritism and obscure patronage. There were some good bosses, and many bad ones. Anyone with an eye for weakness would have seen him coming and had his number at first glance.

There were many light envelopes to come and promises of work to be pulled from under his feet. The kind of everyday exploitation that forms the backdrop to so many immigrant lives, then as now. Was this what he thought things would look like, in his new life? Perhaps this is when his drinking started to escalate, from a weekend ritual to something more obviously problematic. Just one time-worn method of dulling some of the shame of inadequacy and smoothing down the rougher edges of his new reality.

After all, work is one thing; to be endured rather than enjoyed. But home was also a challenge. Those early years before my arrival meant instability and a constant, sometimes grinding precarity. It was hard, for both of them. The constant flitting between Gran's cramped one-bedroom flat on Faversham Road and the homes of other friends and family in the vicinity who could offer shelter for as long as their means or generosity could manage. An existence that still falls under the bureaucratic banner of 'legal homelessness', as it would have done then. My arrival changed all that in the summer of 1992. It's a strange, uniquely gratifying feeling to locate yourself at the heart of your own family's origin story. So much has changed since that it already seems to carry the texture of a childish fable. Almost immediately, Lewisham Council came up with the flat in Hither Green, site of my first hazy recollections and a long hoped-for stable base for my parents to climb clear of their increasingly strained beginnings in the city. The conditions they had dreamed of for so long; a home that could be really theirs, with a new family unit to be grown and nurtured inside it.

And those few years gave them exactly that, or so the most reliable available sources would have it. More coherent thoughts start to surface around this time. Still sporadic, but so often colourful. Clambering over the sofa to sit between them as they watched TV in companionable silence, enjoying devising endlessly convoluted games in the solitude of my room and bringing them out to bear in the safety of the garden, if the weather permitted. The first proper sequence of events I can remember with real precision must have taken place in the autumn of 1996, my first day of nursery in Catford, just a few minutes from home. It's still so vivid, a real electric shock of animation. For the first few minutes, it seemed like the most brilliant adventure; a new space with cheerful, welcoming faces and hand-painted pictures dotting the battered plaster walls of a tumbledown old Victorian house on Rushey Green, the main artery that runs through the area and connects it to the body of Lewisham proper.

The adults were talking in hushed conspiratorial tones, while I slouch in a slightly too big chair, processing all the unfamiliarity and trying to keep my legs from squirming too much, in case I run the risk of a light telling-off from Mum, who is looking more stressed than I can remember seeing her before. I feel myself getting restless, letting my eyes streak about the room, over the same blobs of colour and cracked plaster. It must be home time soon. I want to get back home, to the insanely patterned carpet and treasure trove of cheap plastic toys. But something's wrong. I know when he takes up my hands and says something about being brave. He pulls his eyes to my level, to the point where I can see the brown of them swimming in a sea of yellow. His breath is heavy as he tells me I have to be brave now, because we're coming back this afternoon. But you have to stay here for now, with all the new friends you'll make, he says. Things are blurred after this, but I've no illusions about what it must have looked like; a pathetic scene, full of noisy crying: me, Mum and Christobal. I remember the feeling of helplessness and the dim awareness of a new world I had no choice in joining and being part of, outside the narrow confines of home. The other adult, the teacher, has seen it all a thousand times before and doles out a few professional sympathies. The goodbyes take an age, until the hysteria finally bleeds out, ready for the new day to begin. The last thing I recall from that day is his hands pressed to the window glass from the outside, preparing to turn with a wink and a goofy thumbs up, as his free hand stays clasped in Mum's.

It wasn't long after this that he disappeared from our lives for the first time. It happened just like that. One day he was there, the next day he wasn't, or at least that's how it seemed to me, protected from the context of his vanishing by Mum and the other adults in our life. It was only much later that I grew to understand the reality of what our lives must have been then, outside what I picked up at the time. Something had been wrong and it's possible I felt it even if I can't quite recall all that much of it. But children are perceptive creatures, alert to any changes in atmosphere. I had dimly begun to understand that it wasn't normal; that other dads didn't stay out until the nightmare hours, coming home to be diverted into another room to sleep off the night's excesses. I knew that not all adults carried with them the same almost constant glaze and that they didn't slur their words in the mid-afternoon.

How did it get to the point when the work finally dried up to nothing? How many failures had it taken to make his life feel intolerable? There is no one I know of who can really answer that question yet. Whatever the complex reasons underpinning his decline, everyone agrees on its rapidity. Soon, he was out all night, almost every night. There were arguments and tears, between him and Mum, most often in Spanish, a language I have never been able to speak or understand, despite the heritage my full name implies. Where did he go, on those lost nights? Where did he go, when he vanished that first time? It was only for a few weeks, but I imagine it must have felt like eternity for mum and my extended family. Or perhaps it didn't. She could have been relieved for the respite, from the twin cares of a troublesome husband and a small child. From life lived in a flat that already seemed too small, too tainted by disappointment and tarnished new beginnings.

It was around this time that he'd also run up against the law, over some accusation of now long forgotten petty criminality. It still seems almost inexplicable, that vulnerable, drunken fool thrown into the lion's den against any possible sense of proportion or compassion. But when has either quality been a feature in the life of the poor in this country? Like the stories of so many other people who are continually slipping in and out of sight of their loved ones, there were the moments that must have felt like rock bottom. After a few weeks, he was back, though no one seems to remember exactly how long he was away for. And just a few weeks after that, he was on the move again, fleeing back to Spain. As with so many others that go repeatedly missing, it wasn't the fact that something had changed in his life that caused him to go: it was the fact that nothing had changed at all.

Life carried on. In the spring of 1997, me and Mum moved a few miles up the road to a basement flat in Forest Hill and the start of a temporarily blissful new chapter, marked by a larger back garden and a bedroom I took to be a cavern on first viewing. It didn't matter that there were bars on the windows or the walls were yellowed from second-hand smoke. This was heaven. Just me and Mum tucked in against the roar of the South Circular, only yards from the vast Victorian absurdity of the Horniman Museum. Six months after disappearing to Spain, he returned. Without an explanation or conciliatory words, swaying unsteadily on the doorstep to the flat with a fistful of emaciated plastic flowers, though I don't remember much else aside from a few increasingly vicious rows in Spanish.

He looked bad and almost frightening. His black hair matted with grease, his eyes puffy and red, his skin gaunt from lack of sun; a young man rapidly aged and crumpled before his time. I didn't want to look at him for longer than I could avoid. The spell had broken on his return, even if he rarely spent the night at the new flat. Mum was getting ill. Stress, maybe. You couldn't blame her if that was the case. And people talked; you couldn't expect them to do anything else.

Everything I can honestly write about that time is filtered through the unreliable eyes of childhood. Memories collapse into one another, making strange mosaics out of the vividly remembered and sometimes misremembered fragments. But I know that he was rarely there. There isn't much concrete proof of where he was instead and I'm not even sure it matters too much now. I can know without it being said that it wasn't a place to envy. His absence was one facet of our lives then. We were still real, the two of us, me and Mum, in the little flat with the bars on the windows and the threadbare brown carpet, stretched thin across the floor like dry skin does on bone. But childhood has its own clarity as well as confusions. I can remember the feeling that life was trending downwards into something that didn't have a name yet. There were still plenty of fun, full days, but Mum's face and arms were getting thinner, along with her hair. We still played our games and spent time with our stories, but Mum was tired. Soon enough, Gran would come to stay the night more often. The nights started to feel longer and darker. After a few months, the eyes of other adults began to reflect a horrible sympathy.

And then it happened. Mum died in the autumn of 1999, a few months after my seventh birthday. Breast cancer, barely into her forties. I knew before the adults told me. If I close my eyes I can see it as clearly as if it happened last week, as I sat on the wall in the back garden, looking out into the trees. I just knew, a premonition I suppose. 'Mum's dead, isn't she?' were my first words, as I arrived into a living room full of my ashen-looking relatives. Things were dark for a while and the memories far less abundant.

My new life started, living with Gran and my mum's sister, who moved her life down from Glasgow to look after us both, very young and very old as we were, an arrangement which lasted through a move to Scotland for her work a few years later and ended when I went to university at 18. Christobal was nowhere to be seen. He had taken himself back to Spain, through grief or cowardice, it is impossible to say. This time, he was missing from my life and has remained so ever since, outside of a brief and disastrous visit to La Línea, in 2000. Then, only a long incoherent letter a few years later, posted from a monastery somewhere in northern Spain. He was sorry at the way things had turned out, for him and us. It was an awful thing, but life was messy, he wanted me to understand. It concluded with a few extra platitudes about time healing all things, or whatever. And it's true, for many years I let him drift to the back of my mind, as I got on with all the million other things that got in the way. School, adolescence, house moves, first loves and other griefs. Then university, followed by the start of adulthood and independence. But there has always been the nagging thought that things would have been different, though not better, if he had been here instead of elsewhere. With Mum, I stand in certainty. She is dead, my relations with her frozen in amber. With him, it is different, uncertain, somewhere just out of reach. For many years it's fair to say I didn't really want to know. My life was happy and everything was new and to be explored for the first time. I'm not precisely sure what's changed in the last few years, but something has. Perhaps it's something as superficially arbitrary as an anniversary. The year 2019 was the 20th since Mum's death, and 2020 witnessed the same milestone representing the last time I saw Christobal. It's a strange feeling, though one I feel ready to face up to. After all, I am an adult now, about the same age he was when he took himself back to Spain all those years ago. The cost of not knowing just feels greater now than it used to.

Of the endless unanswered questions that make up a life, there is one that the passing of the years has made the most pressing. It is not just asking who my father was, or perhaps still is. I can already draw a decently complex portrait of him from the remaining, incomplete evidence and the memories of both myself and others who knew him here. The frail young immigrant without the language or networks to express himself or feel comfort, exploited in work and half-drowned under responsibilities he had no idea of how to handle with any kind of success or grace. The irresponsible drunk and addict, as unapologetically selfish as he fancied allowing himself to be on any given day. The vulnerable remand prisoner trapped in a high security hell of killers and thieves. The occasionally present husband and father that wanted to put all the rest of it behind him, without the first clue or understanding of the struggle and sacrifices it would have to take, as well as being somebody else's dysfunctional brother and son, in a place that is still both faraway and strange to me. There is a point to which I can appreciate the complexities of his existence, filtered through the lens of my adult understanding. This is the point at which the whole muddled tapestry can start to make a kind of sense.

It is when I start to try and consider what he is that the whole carefully woven construction starts to unravel to thread in my hands. He is my father; that much is certain. But what else? What more or less? When I think of the man responsible for my existence, I am also considering a ghost, with the proof of his life now little more than a series of yoked-together fragments, to be interpreted with as much generosity as I am capable of. Christobal Garcia-Ferrera has been missing from my life for almost as long as I can remember. To consider him as a missing person is the only thing that really makes any sense to me, though I have only recently begun to understand him in those terms. There will be those who know his fate, but they are missing from me too – my Spanish family, who might themselves have long ago forgotten my own existence.

There's something comforting in the realisation of how few accidents there really are in the patterns that make up one's life. For the last 20 years I have spent many hours contemplating what might have become of Christobal, just as I have spent many weeks and months without him intruding on my thoughts at all. So much has happened, so much time has elapsed and made it all feel so strange, like the half-remembered dreams of another existence; as distant to now as the days before that very first memory from a long-gone summer past.

But here I am, bound on a journey of discovery of his fate, which maybe has no definite, or even desired, conclusion. There is no certainty of what and who might be found. And far beyond my thoughts of him there is the whole shadow world of the missing that I have spent so much time trying to document and make sense of in my professional life as a journalist and writer.

In March 2019, I wrote a long feature for VICE on the current missing persons crises in the UK, in all of its tortured complexity. Christobal was the catalyst that has brought me to the story, however much I initially wanted to believe it otherwise. In the past few years my work has further gravitated to the stories of those slipping out of view, including six months spent reporting on the strange, often poignant case of the still unidentified man calling himself Peter Bergmann, who washed up dead on a beach on the west coast of Ireland after deleting every possible trace of his 'real' identity. I have always tried to remember that the missing are not a homogeneous constituency. By definition, they are hidden from us somewhere just beyond the here and now. They deserve to be treated with dignity, their stories considered just as important as those who remain in sight, however tenuously.

The missing, like the poor, are always with us. And right now we are living in a time and place where their numbers are substantial enough to be deemed a crisis. In the time it has taken you to read these words, more people will have slipped from view. Every year, over 180,000 people are reported missing in the UK, at a rate of one every 90 seconds, according to the most reliable figures compiled by police forces, academics and the dedicated charities working in the field. These are the known missing, the figures whose faces you might even half remember from home-made posters plastered on billboards, bus stops and phone boxes, or desperately shared across social media. Individuals recorded and reported to the police, with family and friends to represent their concerns. Of these missing, many come home, only to vanish again when it's clear that nothing has changed, much like Christobal, all those years ago.

Our culture is full of different representations of the missing, ranging from the high-profile cases that dominate media attention, to the prestige TV dramas that serve as glossy, high-class entertainment. There is the cottage industry of intrigue around certain unsolved cases, like Madeleine McCann or Suzy Lamplugh. Fodder for most macabre and voyeuristic tendencies as readers, viewers, consumers of grief and its mysteries. But these stories represent a tiny fraction of an incomplete picture. Most of the missing are left in silence, far away from the public eye; the many thousands of stories that go untold and are perhaps never even recorded, every year.

The one closest to me tells of Christobal, the wiry spectre with jet black hair, never too far from a joke or nervous collapse. Many of the people that slip through the gaps might have lived in the chaos of dependency. Like him, addicted to drink and substances, or plagued by mental health problems. Many more are failed by structural forces, often far beyond individual control. The safety net that used to exist wasn't perfect, but it has been emaciated down to a trapeze wire over the last decade. The long years of austerity that started with the Conservative/Lib Dem coalition in 2010 has meant less support for the already vulnerable and at risk; less rehab, less access to housing, less mental health treatment and a steep, shocking rise in homelessness. Child poverty rates have dramatically increased over the last decade, with one in four children across the UK living in poverty.[1] None of this was inevitable. It was a choice, just like Christobal's decision to leave was also a choice. Sometimes, the numbers of people reported missing can feel like an impossibility. How can it be true in what is often trumpeted as the most connected era in human history, for so many people to be so perilously at risk from falling out of view? Every day, we are monitored and tracked, our movements apparently mapped out with pinpoint precision by the phones and devices we rely on for so much of our everyday convenience. I don't claim this as anything other than an obvious insight. It's just another fact of the lives we lead in the here and now, one of the ambient absurdities of our time and place. The UK is one of the most surveilled countries in the world, with more surveillance cameras per citizen than anywhere outside of China. Our images are recorded hundreds of times every day, mostly without our consent or knowledge. London alone has around half a million cameras spread out over the city. Of course, they can help with the hunt for the missing. Yet this perpetual churn of recorded data is only so useful. The footage that picks up the last movements of the person on the cusp of disappearing is a guide to their past, not whatever future it is they have been caught heading into. It brings to mind my time spent with the story of Peter Bergmann and his careful movements on the way to his pre-planned death. Having been caught on the CCTV of the hotel he'd checked into in Sligo, he then scrupulously avoided every other camera in town over the subsequent days, the last of his life, while he ran whatever final errands he so desperately wanted to obscure.

The reasons why someone becomes a missing person can be simple, or they can be fiendishly complex. Some will have been taken against their will and marked out for violence. They might have been abducted or killed, with no answers to their fate ever forthcoming. Many more will be alive somewhere, though equally lost. Instances of modern slavery have risen exponentially over the last decade, with over 5,000 cases reported every year though the true number is thought to be far higher. In early August 2020, the BBC reported on the story of Ricardas Puisys, from Wisbech, Cambridgeshire, who had been found alive hiding in the woods five years after he had disappeared at his workplace at a food production company called Nightlayer Leek Company in nearby Chatteris, on 26 September 2015. Police had feared the Lithuanian national had been murdered, even making arrests, though his body had never been located. Ricardas had worked as a casual land worker around Wisbech and lived pay cheque to pay cheque, often changing address at multi-occupancy rentals all around the county. He didn't have a car, or many friends and no immediate family in the UK. His mother lived in Lithuania, his sister in Germany and there were a few cousins scattered about in Ireland. In November 2019, someone had set up a Facebook page in his name accompanied with apparently new images of Ricardas alive after years of silence. Following an extensive search, he had eventually been found in the woods, living heavily concealed in undergrowth. Ricardas had been there a long time, though no one could say exactly how long with any certainty. He had hidden himself carefully and deliberately and hadn't had any human contact for the duration of his time there. Police suspected he had run away from his exploiters, whoever they were. He was being looked after while officers tried to piece together the last half decade, when he had been presumed murdered.

What the dead and the living missing share is this: they are both mostly unknown and unknowable. They are nowhere to us, even if they must be somewhere. There are those that come back, just as there are those that choose to go missing. Most people who go missing or absent themselves don't just do it once, as Christobal didn't. They do it again and again, absconding from family homes and homeless shelters, care homes and mental health wards across the country. The most reliable figures say that up to eight in ten missing adults are living with mental illness, both diagnosed and undiagnosed. Children are more likely to be fleeing violence at home, while at least seven in every ten victims of child sexual exploitation will have also have been the subject of a missing persons report.

The missing tell us about things about society, from their unique place neither quite inside nor outside of it. For many in the UK, life is hard and seems to be getting harder. The cracks are widening and falling between them is much easier than any of us would want to believe. I often think about what it would take, how much or how little it would really need, to slip out of vision. How many months would it take to burn through my own small savings? I am one of the lucky people with a network of friends and a small core of close family who would support me through the worst of any personal crises, at least until they couldn't. It is not something to be taken for granted and who knows what damage the passing of years will do, as it does to so many others.

There are also those that want to leave the bonds of their own existence and claim another brighter one, just beyond the horizon of the here and now. Relationships break down, loved ones die, debts accumulate and deepen, you feel time slipping away, caught in a rut of yours and others making. To become somebody else is a common enough dream and there are those that take it past fantasy, to something concrete. It doesn't always require the forensic attention to deceit you sometimes imagine. It isn't just about shredding your passport or changing your name. It also takes luck, and something like commitment. I suppose Christobal was one of the lucky in his own way. His journey was done in reverse, from the griefs and responsibilities of his new life in London back to the more familiar discomforts of his previous life in Andalusia. It's true that we could have 'found' him, though the possibility began to thin after those early years at the turn of the millennium, after my mother's death. But I've long understood his vanishing as the action of a man who knew it was his only way of exerting control – if control it was – in his own tattered life.

There are many different things that can happen when someone is reported missing. It all depends on who and where. It is often a confusing and sometimes shameful process. It may be that the loved ones of the person are ambivalent in doing so, not out of indifference or spite, but

26

because they distrust authority, or don't know if it's the 'right thing to do'. The charity Missing People define family as something wider than immediate blood ties. They might be anyone with a concern in the wellbeing of the missing person: partners, neighbours, colleagues or friends. To make a report means a degree of scrutiny into the lives of the left-behind. Opening yourself up to it might reveal things you'd rather keep hidden. Having others pour through the contents of your life can be a daunting thing, particularly in times of heightened vulnerability. Some people just want to leave without anything in the way of explanation, or even any clues as to why they've chosen to do what they've done. It made me think of a story I'd heard about before starting work on this book, originating in a Birmingham satellite town in the mid-2000s. A man called John had vanished, if that was even the right word for it. His sister and the extended family didn't think about going to the police until several days after his disappearance and eventually decided against it. He might have deliberately gone, they felt, though they couldn't precisely pinpoint why.

John was always a bit of a local face. He was known in the pubs and social clubs of the town as one of those jovial guys who liked a drink and a flutter, who always had a bit of fresh bravado and liked to hint at the possibility of any new get-rich-quick scheme he and his mates had alighted on. He'd been in a bit of trouble when he was younger. Nothing serious, a few nights in the cells for some drunken scuffles, as well as the time he'd been caught out with some dodgy £20 notes, something he'd always pleaded ignorance about. Bad crowd, wrong place, wrong time. But that had been years ago, he'd been long past all that nonsense. And then one day, he'd stepped out of his house and that was it. He was gone and no one could say where or why. His sister told me that the family felt embarrassed to go to the local police; she knew how they'd pour over the past and use it for their theories. Perhaps he owed money to the wrong person, or had slipped into something deeper. You heard of these things happening. But John was an adult and there was no proof he'd been suicidal, or suffering from any explicit symptoms of crises. His sister told me that there had been a note a few weeks later, reassuring them of his safety and promising he'd be in touch again in due course. It didn't offer much by way of explanation. The promised follow-up didn't materialise and John has never become an open file. He is something else, one of the invisible missing not covered by the official figures or research.

There are also the missing that are defined by their urgency. The cases that involve children or the elderly, or those known to be in acute crises. It might be someone known to be at risk of taking their own life, or a person suffering with dementia who can't quite remember how to make it home safely. They might have wandered, agitated and scared even in what were once familiar settings. It's a question of the risk involved in any particular incident. When they are perceived as high enough, the authorities will treat it with immediate seriousness. Reports will be filed and searches hastily organised. Most British police forces will tell you that this is what they do well. If there is a clear and demonstrable threat to life, the procedures are effective, running along well-worn grooves. These missing are statistically extremely likely to be found, in one form or another. But here, as everywhere, things are changing by necessity, forced by creaking public services and almost a decade's worth of austerity. It's why the conversation on what exactly constitutes a missing person has taken on new life among the professional bodies tasked with their search.

When I started writing this book I wanted to understand some of what lay behind the numbers: the thousands of stories behind the crush of statistics. It didn't seem enough to simply say that one in every 200 children in the UK will go missing every year, with that number standing at one in 500 for adults, even if most of these are the returning missing. I wanted to know where it is that they go when they are missing and all the spaces they might slip through. In London alone, the number of reported missing person cases has increased 77 per cent since 2010,[2] a rate that one senior officer in the city's Metropolitan Police has labelled 'unsustainable', at a time when their already overstretched resources are at breaking point. What can we find out about the lives behind such daunting numbers? What of their families and loved ones left behind? Do we know half as much as we should about the people tasked with searching for the missing? These are some of the questions that have led me to homeless shelters in London and food banks in

Dundee, grieving families in Tyneside and some of the missing who have come back, across the UK. And wherever I found myself, I couldn't shake the thoughts of Christobal and what might have become of him. Soon enough, it will be these same thoughts that lead me back to Andalusia for a final reckoning with his memory, back where it all began for him and my mother, in those distant years passed.

Something I have come to learn in the course of my reporting is never to ask about closure. It is, as one retired detective told me, 'a weak word' and a false promise. It is a question I have tried to avoid asking the many other people I have spoken to, who have lost loved ones or have themselves been missing. Of course, people want answers for themselves and to give to others. But what if they prove to be the wrong ones, the replies that you didn't want to hear? It is a dilemma that is never too far from my thoughts. Searching for the truth can be a risky business, and there is a case to be made that some things should remain out of sight. It's equally plausible that this kind of thought is simply the coward's way out. The truth is often painful and I know that the truth of Christobal's fate is likely to lead me to places I've not always been sure I've wanted to go. But I cannot help feeling that a debt needs to be paid to his story and his memory, just as there is a duty towards the missing more generally. If I know anything at all, it is that the journey towards understanding them both could only have begun in one place, the city which has been home for so much of my life and that proved so unhappy and woven with failure for Christobal. London, or at least the parts of the city that he would have known, has changed almost beyond recognition since those days, in the late 1990s. I've often wondered if he would even recognise the once famil-iar streets two decades later, or if places are liable to vanish just as much as the people who once called them home.

PART II
THE SEARCHERS

CHAPTER 2

Summer felt like an endurance test as I left Vauxhall Underground station on a Tuesday afternoon in June 2019. It was one of those close, grey days in London where the air feels trapped with pollution and tempers are poised on a hair trigger. I was already running as late, due to an earlier signal failure on the Victoria Line. It took a few minutes for my phone signal to reappear so I could double check the address of my destination on my phone. As I walked through the old Pleasure Gardens, there were the last of the office crowd on their lunch hours, trying to soak up the last few minutes of freedom. Tapping at my greasy phone screen, I noticed a couple of tents pitched up at the periphery of the manicured urban greenery, with two youngish men standing close by, smoking warily and asking a few passers-by in pressed blue shirts for change. Earlier in the year I'd read about a new hostel for rough sleepers in the area, opened to some fanfare in December 2018 as part of Lambeth Council's new drive to soothe the effects of rising homelessness in a borough where the number of people bedding down every night on the street is thought to be in the hundreds. Perhaps the men didn't know about it and had pitched up from another area, or they had already been through its doors. I didn't have time to stop and ask.

It felt like the most logical place to begin my journey into the world of those who search for the missing. After around 15 minutes, I found the right alley leading to the entrance of the National Crime Agency offices. It's a strange part of the city, a distended limb on the fringes of southern Zone 1, a stone's throw from a stubbornly unglamorous part of the river, a world of under-occupied luxury flats and pained-looking office complexes: a low-wattage outpost not too far from the heart of the city. It's also where Mum had worked once, in her admin days at Lambeth Council – a time that seemed impossibly remote to me as I made my way down the side streets.

This was to be my first face-to-face meeting with Joe Apps, the head of the UK Missing Persons Unit and a long-time professional in the world of the missing, having started his career working on the Metropolitan Police's first dedicated Missing Unit back in 1995. He came to greet me from reception with a firm handshake before we passed through a maze of thick security doors and surveillance cameras on the way to the unit's home. Before we started, there was a bit of small talk and Joe told me it had been an unusually busy few weeks even by their own standards, as he sought to recruit 15 new members to the team. 'Yes,' he said with half a sigh, 'you could say it's rather a long day already.'

Any weariness either of us felt seemed to melt away even before I put my voice recorder on the table. Joe is an easy man to talk to, something I knew already after a lengthy chat we'd had a few months previously on the phone, several months prior in the early stages of my reporting. Back then, Joe had outlined a bit of his own history with the missing. He'd worked within the NCA since the unit's formation in 2008, after it was set up to succeed its predecessor in the Met. He told me how the UK once led the way in the hunt for missing people, with the world's first bureau set up in London in 1929; by 1994, every European nation had its own dedicated unit. There are three basic functions, he had explained then and was reiterating now: 'To take on both missing person and found person cases from local police forces; to add value to existing investigations by providing support and expertise; and to use the data we receive to draft an annual statistical report on the number of missing and found people, which is then published online as the Missing Persons Data Report.'

Another crucial part of their work revolves around trying to match 'found people' to the legions of the missing on file. These are the people who return from missing episodes, for whatever reason. '[The police] will often get in touch and ask if we have any found people on our records that match the description. We'll look, but it's not often we do. Usually it's a dead person, or a person in hospital with amnesia, which we then have a higher success rate in matching.'

Joe and his team work in a world of shadows; hunches, glimpses and half-clues to be pieced together in the hope of what? Providing reconciliation and closure to the lives of those touched by the disappeared. But underpinning it all is a simple moral issue – a duty towards the missing. When the records had transferred over from the Met in 2008, they noticed around 800 unidentified people listed. That number had now been reduced to about 600, 100 of whom are babies – foetuses, newborns or infanticide victims. Another hundred are cases where a missing person abroad is thought to have a UK connection. The rest are outstanding warrants; dead bodies in the UK. 'A number that is still far too high for our country and society,' he'd added quietly.

My first impressions of Joe in the flesh were the same they had been when talking on the phone – a man who intimately knew both his subject and how to communicate it clearly and without exasperation when greeted with a layman's questions. In my naivety, I thought I'd already known something about the world of missing people. A personal hunch, formed by my own tangled thoughts of Christobal and fleshed out by my early and piecemeal reading and reporting. But here was someone who had devoted their life to an issue that has always been with us and appeared to be deepening in severity. His expertise started to feel like it could only show up my enthusiasm as amateurish in comparison.

I needn't have worried. Face to face, Joe is a cheerful, reassuring presence. The sort of man that has a kind word for everyone, quite willing to indulge someone writing a book and armed with all sorts of abstract questions. Though the cases could be gruelling, he doesn't really do despair or affect world-weary fatalism. There is far too much work to be done for that. Over our first cup of tea, Joe wanted to start with one of the biggest questions: What is a missing person? It's a question with immediate significance. The definition is something that is constantly tweaked, refined and batted between the various agencies with a stake in the missing. In his view, the current wording is too wide and places too much stress on depleted police resources. '[At the moment] it lets everyone become reported as a missing person without regards to their vulnerability, or the right to be forgotten. And we should also be asking, does the person really want to be found?' For Joe and others that share his thinking, this comes to a question of fundamentals. 'Many people who go missing don't think they're missing at all, because they don't have that concept in their head. The family might think one way. They might well be distraught. But if that person is an adult – like your dad – then you have to say, well, they have every right to do what they want, even to the point of disregarding family emotions. In a case where there's no vulnerability, the police will take a report, but they'll also say that they aren't going to put resources into it. Particularly in the case of a family estrangement or something of that ilk.'

Over the hours that we spoke, it's clear that Joe enjoys an anecdote and he offered one up to illustrate the daily dilemmas faced by families and police. The previous weekend, he'd been round at a friend's house in Ascot, the small east Berkshire town. One of their neighbours had come round, in a state of panic. The woman's 15-year-old grandson was out with a friend in nearby Camberley, hanging about the town centre in the usual time-honoured way of teenagers across the country. They had phoned to ask if they could stay the night, to save themselves an evening trip back to Ascot. Yes, that was fine, according to their grandmother. By 10 p.m., they hadn't arrived home. She phoned their father, who was soon going apoplectic wondering where his teenage daughter could be. Anger quickly turned into concern as more and more time passed in silence. Soon, they were crossing the invisible line, where their daughter was becoming a missing child, rather than just a teenager that isn't in the place they're supposed to be. When does the family start to report to the police? Was it 10 p.m. when they start to notice they haven't turned up at the grand-mother's house? Was it 11.30 p.m., just before both of them actually turned up sheepishly at the grandmother's door? It later transpired that the daughter had been in contact via text, but had 'turned her phone off after some threatening texts from Dad, telling them that they were grounded for a year, and that sort of thing,' Joe outlined with a laugh. The question is: when would they have become a missing person? 'The police will say that they can't see any risk, at that point. Do the family even want the police intrusion into their lives? Many don't, for whatever reason. People often decide that they can handle it themselves. The police are in a similar position; perhaps they don't want to make that report because it isn't a serious enough case.'

What exactly constitutes a serious enough case, I wanted to know. When the 'missing' definition was changed in 2013, it was to a strict 'harm-based definition', something that charities and law enforcement alike thought too rigid. It was widened and complicated in 2016 with the new category of 'no apparent harm', which means the recipient is still logged as a missing person, even though they are not thought to be under immediate risk – something most agree is now too broad. It's a sub-clause that will have an impact on the new figures that are set to be published at the end of the year, which are expected to show a 25 per cent increase in the number of reported missing cases. For police forces across the country, missing is not simply an ethical question. It is something concrete and pressing. Searching is expensive and time consuming; just one of the hundreds of daily responsibilities to be shared around and gnawing at the sides of every working day. The past decade has witnessed much talk about cuts to policing budgets, usually in relation to a perceived rise in crime that comes with it, though it's hardly a straightforward or undisputed connection. Between March 2010 and March 2018, police forces in England and Wales lost 21,732 officers, an overall drop of 15 per cent,[3] to the lowest numbers since 1981. Austerity was the rationale, part of the Cameron/Osborne deficit reduction pathology. In Scotland and Northern Ireland the picture is slightly different, with numbers staying relatively stable over the same period, though there were the first signs of decline and, in Scotland's case, the administrative chaos of the 2013 Police Scotland merger which saw all eight of the country's regional forces swallowed into one central command.

It seemed to me to translate into a reality where anything deemed non-essential has been slashed to the bone, or jettisoned entirely. There are tales of officers developing post-traumatic stress disorder (PTSD) from working alone, with the strain and stress of the job proving too much to cope with. Despite Boris Johnson's autumn 2019 pledge to recruit 20,000 more police officers in three years, little seems to have changed in the meantime, with many forces fearing a further wave of cuts after the enduring impact of coronavirus.

What the cuts have created is a world where the borderline missing inevitably slip down the pile, with a strategic need to prioritise caseloads. More open files mean more unwanted scrutiny and pressure from the higher-ups. A possible child abduction will always be a matter of urgency in a way that a child who has broken curfew, or an adult choosing to up and leave won't. The fact is, as Joe put it, that demand has to be reduced from a policing perspective. 'For the limited resources they do have, they need to be concentrated on the cases that the police can solve, and the ones they should solve. Of course, these are two very different things.' Though it doesn't diminish the pain felt by the left-behind, as Joe is readily aware. Even in the early 2000s, the idea that we would have taken Christobal's case to the police would have seemed laughable. There was nothing much to report. He left, we lost contact and it was left to deaden to silence, until we made a choice to move on. The question of urgency didn't enter into it, though it didn't diminish the hurt done. What, I asked Joe, is there to be done in these cases, when the family still want to try and establish contact outside of the police channels.

'[It's difficult because] they're still stuck. The person is missing, the police won't help and they can't get anyone else to find him either. They might resort to charities or churches and other tracing agencies. When someone is reported missing and they're then found as an adult, the first thing they'll ask is "What do you want us to tell your family?"' Joe explained. The response is not always the one that the families want to hear. 'Sometimes it's "Tell them I'm safe and well", sometimes they don't want anything said at all because it's something in the family that's generated the missing episode in the first place. So this notion of "What's a missing person?" is a question that's becoming more fundamental in both academic and practical thinking.'

It's a conversation as varied as the people who comprise the missing, but I wanted to stay on the left-behind for a minute. The not knowing can drive people to extremes. The families that clamour for police attention have a strong view, but there are also those who eventually give up the search. The effects ripple out in unexpected ways and previously unshakable relationships are altered in ways you never thought possible.

As Joe said to me about an hour into our meeting, it's not a good or a bad thing. It's just a fact. Some people are more resilient than others and others can't really can't cope without a lot of assistance. The idea of 'invisibility' is a powerful thing. He explained how the process of reporting someone missing to the state is itself a kind of trauma. The transformation of a person into a record can be difficult to deal with. One person's entirety reduced into a two-page report in a filing cabinet. It's something I often think of Christobal. He still exists in my mind, even if just as an apparition: a weedy, sallow figure in a cheap leather jacket poised somewhere on the outskirts of my memory. He has never quite been fully inducted into the shadow world of the missing, though I'm not sure I could explain why the distinction matters. Not yet, at least. The possibilities of his fate are just about endless, even if I still thought most of them to be little more than useful delusions.

Much has changed over the course of Joe's long career. The advent and inexorable rise of social media is by no means the least significant development. In the before times, appeals were limited to posters and old-fashioned police work. That's what it took when it was done right, going door to door, building a methodical portrait of the person that had gone; their habits and haunts. The places they'd go and friends they trusted, or might have fled to. And if police interest waned, it would be up to the families or loved ones to keep the flame alive, with handmade efforts stuck to lampposts and bus stops for as long as the paper held – sometimes desperate pleas with phone numbers scrawled across them with the hope of something, anything, to keep them going in the search.

It feels silly to even recall when faced with the weight of the missing, but I remember back in 2002, not too long after Mum had died and Christobal had left, how Gran had painstakingly crafted a little poster for our missing cat who we had christened Socks on account of his white paws set against his sleek black fur. It doesn't sound like much but I remember her artistry and the thought that, even back then, just how unlikely it was that someone would see the neatly clipped little photo framed by her distinctive looping script stuck jostling for space on the notice board at the Sainsbury's in Forest Hill. I still have the appeal in a drawer somewhere, a memory of Gran after her passing in 2009 and of those long forgotten days, even if Socks never did come home alive.

Things are different today. Joe told me how it's a myth he's always rubbing up against, that the internet has given birth to a connectedness that makes it somehow less easy to go missing. It isn't anything like the whole picture, in his view. 'It might be Twitter or Facebook or whatever else. You have these friends on it and some of them will be your friends. But there are others that you don't know all that well. If you were to drop out of sight, how long would it really take [them] to notice?' They are also platforms that offer another means to search for those that have left, as I'd found out over long months of researching and reporting. I've spent more time than is probably healthy scrolling down the manifold Facebook pages devoted to the hunt for the missing. They all share a texture, a specific pitch, an urgent frequency. There are dozens of them, created from all around the UK. Some focus on a specific case, run by the loved ones of whoever it is that's missing. They have the feeling of a mosaic, a careful patchwork of details and dense information. Often, they're refreshed daily, which keeps the case circulating around people's newsfeeds. The saddest ones are those where the updates have dropped off, from a lack of information or perhaps just despondency. Dead pages, the last post from the mid-2010s, weighted down with a grim kind of inevitability.

A few months after I met Joe in the autumn of 2019, I found myself added into one for a middle-aged man named Pete Brown who had gone missing that same year. Every day, there would be the same appeals sent out to the group. He'd last been seen near Whitby and had gone missing from a mental health unit where he was being treated for depression. There was still hope, after a chain of sightings of a hunched man with a self-fashioned walking stick, including one of a man who fitted Pete's description who had been seen walking down the A1079 road, on the way to Hull. It could have been him, but the witness couldn't really say with any certainty. The man was wearing a cap and it was hard to see his face. Pete had last been seen in a blue hoodie underneath a blue waist-length jacket, loose grey cotton jogging bottoms and blue Nike trainers, and might have been wearing a blue baseball cap. By mid-2020, when I was in the group, it was clear his family were distraught – the pain amplified with each week and month that Pete was still lost to them. I'd messaged an intermediary who helped run the group to see if they might be willing to talk to me. It wasn't a cruel request, I hoped, as they had spoken to some local press about the case and I wondered if further coverage might help. The family's response was a polite no and I picked up on the feeling that there was no point going through it all again, while they were still living through all the uncertainty.

Other groups are different, focussed more on the missing crisis more generally: a mass of posts and appeals ranging from missing teenagers who have absconded for the weekend to long-term 'mispers' and older people who might be living with dementia, who have wandered from their home or secure accommodation. There are even a few cases that can't help but raise a smile. I'd noticed several from a particular kind of older person, trying to track down a girl or boy they'd once had an unforgettable dance with, all the way back in their gilded youths. No, they didn't have a photo, an address or even a name, but they did have that memory, if anyone could help locating the girl with the pearly smile and long red hair who had been at the Barrowlands Ballroom on that balmy June night in 1964. But mostly, it was the same sad tale. Just sometimes you could see a story solved in real time. The missing person would turn into a found one, usually after a couple of days or so – the window of time that most people who come back come back within.

It didn't take long to feel strange, lurking around these pages that seemed to exist in the same space as the missing themselves. So many stories, so many faces and people left in limbo behind them. I thought of the admins, specifically one woman in one of the largest groups, who seemed to be posting relentlessly every day. Thankless work, I thought to myself, done at a seemingly impossible pace. In another, I got speaking to a woman with a missing brother in Ayrshire, who had been waiting for his return for almost 20 years. We even set a date to talk in person, in early 2020, but as the date rolled round she'd messaged to say the police advised against it, as the case was still technically lying open. It just seemed to confirm something I'd started to feel about the groups. For some, they were clearly useful supplements in the search for the missing, to boost support when the authorities didn't have the time or inclination to give the needed support. For others, they seemed to almost be a trap. A constant reminder of their loss and a space that only seemed to deepen the purgatory they'd been forced to live in. When I spoke to Joe Apps about them he was cautious not to come down too hard on either side. They can, he said, be a force for good. Long before I started writing this book, I'd felt an odd pang when I saw the latest appeals being circulated on Twitter with thousands of retweets, flung across the outer reaches of the platform. The impulse is to share. It makes you feel like you're doing something, that you're part of a noble cause to help locate someone who has slipped out of sight. The lost teenager's face staring back at you from a grainy JPEG screenshotted from their social media profiles, along with the police or family appeal itself. No context, no knowledge of the person behind the plea. Just another figure to be found.

Our tea had long got cold by the time we returned to the question of what makes a missing person. It isn't just law enforcement that has a stake in the definition. Charities are liable to think differently from police forces and the discussions tend to be robust. It is not just a UK-wide question, with any international consensus just as far out of reach, according to Joe. Missing People is the best-known missing charity in the UK, set up in April 1993 to counter what was then an unprecedented rise in the number of disappearances. Their remit is both narrower and wider than Joe's and encompasses what law enforcement often can't. They are not strictly investigators, though they run hundreds of appeals for information on individual cases and share their work with local authorities and police forces. Their sole responsibility is to the missing and the left-behind, a sometimes uneasy coalition whose interests don't always neatly align.

If you live in one of the UK's major cities or towns, then you're likely to have seen one of their appeal posters dotted around train stations and bus stops. They're designed to grab attention, to highlight the scale and intensity of the crisis at hand. Will you help us find every child, they ask in bold block lettering in white and black, set against a red banner. Many of them use the face of Andrew Gosden to add to the appeal. The then 14-year-old had left his home in Doncaster on 14 September 2007 and travelled by train to King's Cross station in London, after withdrawing £200 from his bank account. He'd been wearing black jeans, a black Slipknot t-shirt and a black canvas satchel with band patches woven onto the fabric and had on his usual distinctive prescription glasses. His fringe was swept down his forehead in the particular goth style of the mid- to late 2000s. The last confirmed sighting of Andrew was at 11.25 a.m. that same morning, as he was captured on CCTV walking out of the main entrance at King's Cross. To this day, his fate is still unknown. He hadn't been a particularly troublesome teenager and there weren't any significant clues that his life was leading to a disappearance. He was a bright lad, a good student with a 100 per cent attendance record at school – a shy, thoughtful kid who teachers described as having a maturity beyond his years. The whole story is a mixture of baffling loose ends and random detail. Perhaps he'd met someone on the internet, who had convinced him to make the trip down, but no hard evidence was ever found to support this hypothesis. In the year following his vanishing, there were over a hundred sightings reported to police from all over the country. Some were wild and others more plausible. His family held on to one in particular that seemed more likely than the rest, that of a boy who matched Andrew's description in a Pizza Hut on Oxford Street, the day of his disappearance. The timings made sense, but didn't lead to anything, just as another sighting in Covent Garden later that day didn't seem to go anywhere. The family have since criticised the Met and what they perceived as an ineffectual response. For instance, the woman who reported the Covent Garden sighting wasn't interviewed until six weeks after Andrew's vanishing, along with a catalogue of other errors. It's the sort of story that stays imprinted at the front of your mind right after first reading. In 2008, a man pressed the intercom outside a police station in the West Midlands and told them he had information about Andrew Gosden. It was verging into night, so the door to the reception was locked. By the time an officer arrived to take his details the man had vanished and has never been traced, despite urgent subsequent police appeals. Months have passed into years and there are still occasional sightings. There are computer-generated likenesses of what he might look like now, as a fully grown man – taller, with shorter hair or more modern glasses. And still, his family waits, hoping for the key to turn in the door and their son, their brother to return home, where his room still sits undisturbed from the day of his vanishing.

The use of Andrew Gosden's image isn't just about raising awareness for the missing. Missing People also offers a tracing service called Lost Contact, for those looking to search for their missing loved ones, quite aside from what the police might be able to promise or prioritise. Though the charity is based in central London, the focus is on the whole of the UK, even if resources are often stretched. There is a small core team of staff and a dedicated cadre of volunteers to support them, mainly with the hunt for the missing. If there is a 'frontline' in the missing persons crisis, then they are on it, all year round. There isn't a quiet time or off season in their line of work, which ranges from academic research to the pressing, practical business of their day-to-day work. The clock doesn't stop on the missing.

I'd wanted to talk with the charity for a long time, even before this book was a reality. If nothing else, I wondered if they might be able to steer me on the right path if I ever wanted to try and trace Christobal. Months had passed since my meeting with Joe, when I spoke with Kirsty Hillman who runs Lost Contact. It was a very different experience to my meeting with Joe in the NCA office, though Kirsty was just as easy to speak to – another dedicated professional who took my questions in good grace and steered me around the work they do and all the manifold things that go into it. The Zoom link cracked slightly at the start of our chat, a new occupational hazard during some of my reporting in 2020. If the workload was challenging before, it had ramped up another gear with the pandemic, she told me. That was true for her part of the charity, though the entire operation was even busier than usual. '[Though] I think what I do has been impacted in another way, on another level, because there's so much anxiety around. People are feeling a sudden urgency to know where their loved ones are. It's about 50 to 60 per cent busier than before. It's a big jump. Obviously I used to have volunteers who worked with me and we've lost them at the moment, though I hope they'll return [at some point].' Kirsty, like her colleagues, was also working from home – an operational challenge in a job that requires so much face-to-face contact, with co-workers as well as those who she is helping search for their loved ones. It can be 'interesting', to use Kirsty's euphemism, with her own small children in the house. 'Some of the conversations I have can be very long and complex and there are hair-raising moments when you feel you might be interrupted. It is what it is,' she added with a smile.

Kirsty is younger than Joe and hasn't spent as much time immersed with the missing. She joined Missing People in early 2017, after a prior career in events. Originally, she'd been in a fundraising role before a new job came up in the relaunched Lost Contact service. Its appeal was immediate. 'I thought it was fascinating and wanted to get more frontline experience. I've been in the role for over a year now. [One of] the things that surprised me when I started was the sheer volume of issues and just how broad they were. It can feel like every other issue feeds into missing.' After the new General Data Protection Regulation (GDPR) guidelines introduced in 2018 meant that the service had to radically change. Previously, they'd been able to hold information without the express consent of the person being looked for. As the law shifted, this was no longer possible, Kirsty explained. 'For instance, I'd ask you about your dad and he hasn't authorised me [to hold that information]. Rather than take any risks with that, we decided to close the service for about a year and a half. The relaunch was just to make sure we were protecting that data and doing it right.' It was also a chance to expand what they had offered, an opportunity as well as a constraint. Previously, the service was exclusively for people that had been in contact over the previous 15 years. It now stands at 20. They've also secured a new funder, 'which is fantastic', Kirsty added. Though she still sits within Missing People, her payroll comes from a corporate sponsor. 'These were major, fundamental changes. I came in to run the service, as someone solely dedicated to it, instead of other people chipping in [along with] their other roles.'

Missing People aren't alone in offering a tracing service. There are others that have more money and resources. '[For example] the Salvation Army's is huge,' Kirsty explained. Though she was happy to tell me about Missing People's process, some things have to remain confidential, like the names of the professional bodies they work with. Before they begin there are also criteria that need to be met before a case gets taken on. Firstly, there has to have been some contact in the last two decades. It has to have been what is called substantial contact: they have to have met and have had a relationship of some kind. Practically speaking, there are also necessary details: a full name, a date of birth, the last known address. These are key. The person being searched for has to be over 18, as does the person looking. They have to be, or thought to be, in the UK. There can't be a legal reason preventing contact. After that, there is an online application to be filled in, though for those that can't, the option is there to do it over the phone. At that point, Kirsty will assess the data and come back with a list of questions, trying to get to the bottom of their circumstances. 'I'm trying to get as much information as possible, red flags as well as anything that might help me [in the search]. We go through all of that and if everything fits then we'll take on the case and send over a pledge that just gives a bit of understanding about how we work.' One of the most common mistakes by applicants is the idea that Missing People can enforce contact, just as Joe had said about the NCA's work. 'People might think we can just hand over an address and say "here you go". It's something I spend a lot of time with,' Kirsty added, 'trying to explain that we will only put people in contact if the person that is being looked for wants it. There are quite a lot of ifs and that can be tough for families. Particularly when it's a parent looking for a child – an adult child – of theirs. They just want to know if they're ok and it can be hard for them to accept that there might be no answer at all.' Andrew Gosden's family came straight to mind. The decade and more of pain and ambiguity: the kind of grief to make your blood run cold. There is also the question of time in Kirsty's work. Sometimes the search might take a week, it might take up to a year, with no guarantee of success. There is also bad news to deliver and sometimes the worst. 'We get a certain amount of death notifications which we then need to relate back,' she explained carefully. 'It's about preparing people for the possible outcomes.'

That doesn't just mean death. It applies to those who are found, just as readily. 'The return might still be a very traumatic and upsetting experience. I think sometimes there is a lot of courage in knowing that it might be right not to be in touch, which is really hard. [Coming back] isn't the end of the story. I see that more and more. It's a very brave decision. If someone has had their lives turned upside down, then sometimes it might not always be the right answer. The old me might never have said that before starting this job.'

The world of the missing is rarely simple, for those on either side of its divide, the lost and those left in their shadow. Of course, the desire to know is a powerful thing, perhaps one of the most powerful and painful needs to live with. 'If only I knew' is a common refrain and one I'm all too willing to admit has been a bigger part of my own life than I occasionally care to imagine. But it isn't the kind of knowledge that solves the tangles of what led to his absence in the first place. It isn't a magic bullet, fired to fix his struggles with drink, or win his other myriad battles. 'It's never as simple as that when you're looking at addiction, or homelessness, or debt and mental health. There are so many things. It just doesn't end there,' as Kirsty added.

As well as the difficulties, it's important to remember the successful reconnections, of which there are many in amongst all of the false starts and thwarted leads. They are the reason Kirsty does the job she does. There is no other feeling that quite compares to it. At the time of our talk, she had 130 open files to work through, with some needing more support and attention than others. There are often surprises: the cases that remain stamped vividly on the imagination. Recently, Kirsty reunited a brother and sister who hadn't seen each other in two decades. 'I received an email saying that yes, he wanted to be put in contact, and that was amazing. After that, I had an email from her, saying they'd just lost another relative who had passed away a few months before. The things she said made me cry, they were so wonderful. That I could have no idea how much we'd changed her life. I've spoken to her on the phone every day since. She got to tell their elderly mother that her son was back. I can't imagine another job where you get the experience of hearing that and being able to play a part in it. It's the best feeling in the world.'

Kirsty is under no illusions about the emotional pull her work holds, for herself as well as the people who she is trying to help. 'Just before Christmas, we had a son who was looking for his mother and we reconnected them. The message I had from her was that she had been having suicidal thoughts and that the reconnection had essentially saved her life. You can't quite believe the honour of being the person who helps to make that happen.' The question of support is always somewhere near the surface, with the tracing process apt to stir up dormant fears in both the searcher and the searched for, like another recent case of an elderly father looking to contact his son. It's natural that people get worried about blame and questions about the past, some of which can never be answered or addressed to anyone's satisfaction. 'The son wrote a message to me that he wanted to be passed to his dad and there was no way I could have read it over the phone, it was so moving. Instead, I posted it to him. I've had a few messages from the dad since, saying how happy he was and that the fear he had is gone now.' I hadn't really thought too much about that fear yet. It isn't a word I've ever had too much use for, when it comes to Christobal. After we spoke, I realised that their criteria meant that I couldn't take his case to Kirsty at Missing People, even if I decided I wanted to. Though it was just within the 20-year limit, I didn't have a reasonably accurate last address and knew that if he was anywhere, he was almost certain to be in La Línea and not in the UK. From the start I'd thought about what a reunion would look like. How it could play out as farce. Him in his broken English, me with my non-existent Spanish, relying on gestures and body language, both equally incapable of putting the point across with any clarity. And if by chance the barriers to communication were levelled, what could we say to one another that wouldn't immediately stiffen to embarrassed silence? Where to even begin, catching up with half a lifetime's worth of mystery and unsaid things.

CHAPTER 3

Alan Rhees-Cooper is not a man who has any difficulty making himself understood. The veteran police officer spent decades working in West Yorkshire, eventually rising to the rank of chief superintendent. Of those long years, many were spent solely dedicated to the missing. When we spoke a few weeks after my long talk with Kirsty at Missing People, I wanted to understand something of his long career and try to soak up a different perspective on the missing.

Alan is now Staff Officer to the National Police Chiefs Council's Lead for Missing People, a job that involves plenty of research and participation on the question of what exactly constitutes a missing person. Though Alan has spent a significant chunk of his over-30-year career in policing working with the missing, he told me it had started as little more than a happy accident. In 2004, Alan took up a development post at West Yorkshire Police, 'to develop his strategic thinking,' as he explained to me. 'There was this big file on the shelf that said "missing people project". They were looking for something for me to do, so I waded through that and made a number of recommendations on how to change the police response to missing people and how to improve it.' One of the key takeaways was that a dedicated missing persons coordinator was needed, who could drive their work throughout the force. For his bosses, there was an obvious candidate: Alan. 'They just said ok, that's your job. I did that all the way through into 2011. I still did all the training until 2017, when I was promoted to chief inspector.' Just before Alan was due to retire, the national role presented itself. 'I retired for about five weeks. It's full time, but I'd be happy to do it for a few more years.'

It was obvious just a few minutes into the interview that Alan was sceptical about the idea of a missing persons crisis. When I asked if he thinks things have got worse over his long career, the response was sudden and direct. 'No, I don't think there's any grounds to believe that the numbers of missing people have fluctuated. There's plenty of evidence to show the changes in police recording practices have [made the figures change].' Alan pointed to the numbers of people reported missing from hospital to argue his point. 'This is something else we're trying to change. When a patient leaves hospital before their treatment is over, they often get reported missing to the police. Now we know that most of these individuals go home. It's been a practice for years that we record them as missing. But the reality is they are not a missing person. If they've gone home, then they aren't missing.' What he was trying to say, he added, was that 'unless there is a real, immediate and substantial risk to life, then don't ring the police. The cases [in the healthcare context] we want to know about are if that person is waiting for a mental health assessment and is now off to commit suicide. Or an older person with dementia who can't make their way home.' The police have a limited, specific function, he told me. If it's a medical issue, it should be an ambulance that deals with it. If it's a mental health issue it should be, in an ideal world, mental health services who deal with it. 'We are not trained in mental and physical health in the same way that these other bodies are. It's a bit like if you had a water leak, would you ring the police? We aren't the experts.' It's a point that would crop up time and again in my journey through the world of the missing. Though the police are useful when a case clearly involves criminality, they aren't who you'd want a response to a mental health crisis or the sensitive work of reintegrating someone who had returned back into the often fraught lives they'd left behind.

In speech and manner, Alan couldn't be more different to Joe Apps, who had been my first route into the law-enforcement side of missing. Where Joe had been softly spoken, Alan talked quickly with a blunt undertone, as might be expected from a career police officer. Though generous with his time, there was the feeling of a man who didn't suffer fools gladly and wouldn't mind telling you that to your face. 'The reality is that the real number of missing people is far less than the numbers shown. A lot of people are recorded as missing who shouldn't be. If you look at your history, there was a dip [in the number of people reported missing] through 2004–2012. Then we started recording everybody as missing and we're trying to get it back in the middle.' Alan also didn't appear too keen on the use of social media to drum up publicity. It can be harmful, he added, its implications both long term and potentially unalterable. 'You can't get rid of that social media footprint. We've had people who are ten years on from a few missing episodes. A conscientious employer will google them and see them as unreliable or unstable. We've had people who say their prospects have been seriously damaged by that. And they don't think of themselves as missing. They feel really aggrieved. It's another thing that we have to consider … sometimes the comments under [our own] appeals are so nasty and destructive that we've had to take them down.'

Again, we were back at the right to be forgotten. He used an example that described my predicament with Christobal down to a fine point, perhaps inadvertently on Alan's part. 'If I fall out with my family and start a new life somewhere else. If the police are constantly looking for me when I've done nothing wrong, then why? There's that other tension with long-term missing adults.' It's hard to gather leads, even if they want to. Banks won't cooperate for financial records, mobile-phone suppliers won't hand over the data, as the risk isn't high enough. The NHS won't hand over records if the person has registered with a GP in a new part of the country.

'We're not a tracing agency and too often we're looking for people we shouldn't be,' Alan emphasised. 'Our job is just to do that initial investigation to see if there are any suspicious circumstances. Is there grounds to believe they're a victim of crime, or might have killed themselves or had an accident up on the Moors? Once we've eliminated those things, that's not a police responsibility.' Our lives are full of risk, he said – it was just about the way you managed it.

So what about the cases where the police did continue to play a part, I wanted to know, where someone was, in his view, genuinely missing. How did the police go about their jobs then? There are a few things that stay consistent, he replied. First, officers will check with friends, relatives and associates and do an address check. Then there are the places typically frequented by the missing person. 'That might be a favourite location, a reservoir or place in the countryside. With young people, it might be somewhere in the city centre. If someone has a vehicle we can check number-plate recognition systems to see if we can locate it anywhere. Then we have checks around mobile phones. If they've left it behind then we can check who they've contacted. And if this person has started a new life somewhere else, what other agencies can we involve in that.' There are checks to be run against the force's own intelligence databases and sometimes forensic searches to carry out. Depending on the severity of the case there might be 20 officers working on it, some drafted in from other districts. On others, it will be the responsibility of a single officer, working alone and juggling the responsibility with whatever other work they have on.

From Alan and Joe who had spent their careers in law enforcement to Kirsty at Missing People, I'd started to glean an important series of insights into the methods of those searching for the missing and the sort of temperament it took to do the jobs they did. Naturally enough, the three of them had differing opinions and methods. They approached my questions from different angles and spoke to their own particular sets of expertise. What united them wasn't just their concern for locating the missing. They all worked from a baseline of public service. The duty was to the missing, to make sure they were found safely – if they wanted to be found at all. There was a moral sense underpinning their work, a carefully set contract of rules and ethics to follow.

My last part of my journey into the world of the searchers was slightly different. It took a long time to find a private detective who would talk to me. Months melted past and the list of rejections had fattened into a book of its own. I tried to understand, to put myself in their position. Why would they want a writer sniffing around their business and peeking into the shadow world they'd chosen to work in? Mostly, they were polite, almost to a fault. There were a few baffled secretaries who promised a call back that never materialised, but mainly it was a variation of the same prompt email reply. No, they usually opened, we wouldn't be interested in talking with you about your book. As one put it bluntly enough, 'We don't talk to the media.'

Alright, I thought, fair enough. Or at least, that's what passed through my mind during the early months of writing. Most of the websites had left me with a grubby feeling that was hard to shake. The comfortingly clean, reassuringly bland professional portals, gleaming with testimonials from satisfied customers. They could have been for any local plumbing firm or trusted family-run accountant, except these messages had a slightly different tone that it took a while to place: an occasionally unsettling cocktail of surveillance and domestic intrusion.

One agency offered the rental of a tracking device, to stick to the bottom of a car for the apparently reasonable rate of £100/hour. Others offered a missing person's tracing service, without any of the carefully ethical patchwork of Missing People or the Salvation Army. Mostly, however, the reviews seemed to come from vindicated spouses who had hired a detective to prove their partner's infidelity. They weren't precisely the kind of domestic dramas I was looking for. Though the more I read, it would be a lie to say I wasn't interested in their services, at least hypothetically. Of course, there was curiosity, sprung from an adolescence spent with too many detective novels. I wondered what it would feel like to hand over a Christobal dossier in a dank basement office, full of yellowed papers and faded Polaroids, to a cynical old PI with tobacco-stained fingers and the same hangdog visage as Gene Hackman in *The Conversation*. It was a fantasy image, almost laughable in its tangle of banal Hollywood cliché.

The false starts and thwarted leads kept accumulating. Just getting past first base felt like an achievement. The website for UKPI (UK Private Investigators) claimed they could generally trace anyone in the world within 24 hours. I loaded up the online live chat and typed a greeting. After a polite, if brisk, back and forth I said I was interested in their work with missing people. 'I am sorry, I cannot discuss employment on here,' came the response, before the UKPI representative abruptly left the chat. A few weeks later, I'd rang another of the top searches that came up in my Google search for a London-based PI. Within seconds, I found myself connected with a representative, a woman with a kind voice and a soft Northern accent who talked me through some of their services. She asked for a few details, a name, if I had a last address and what the circumstances were. Was he missing in the legal sense, or would it be fair to say we were just estranged? How old were you when he left? I tried to keep the details as close as possible to my chest, but let slip that his name was Garcia. 'Ok, right,' she'd replied, 'the surname isn't too bad. I'd hope that this would be straightforward, with nothing too sinister or complex. I would think you'd come in for a standard trace fee.' That would come to £350 plus VAT, half up front, half on completion. It sounded like the simplest thing in the world, as if she was quoting the price on a monthly payment plan for a new Vauxhall Corsa. I could expect results in around 14 days if the case was as bog standard as it sounded and could be reassured by their 95 per cent success rate. There wasn't much more to say, so I thanked her for her time and help, before cutting off the call. I'm not sure precisely why or how it made me feel so strange. There was, as the flurry of websites I'd read made crystal clear, nothing illegal about their endeavours. But I couldn't imagine the idea of discovering Christobal's fate that way, or feel well disposed to the idea of the hunt for the missing boiled down to a transaction. It might have had something to do with vanity. It can be hard to admit that the major events of your own life might not carry the same boundless fascination subjected to the glare of the outside world. There is nothing quixotic about a bank receipt showing a transfer to a company with a bland, scrupulously discreet name, for services rendered in locating a man who has been missing from your life, for almost as long as you can remember. And there was still a part of me that wanted to find something thrilling at the end of my journey. Some final, cinematic flourish that would make sense of everything I'd ever doubted and misunderstood about our shared past.

After the call, I'd had enough for that particular day, so I left my desk and decluttered my mind with some domestic chores instead. From Joe at the National Crime Agency, to Kirsty at Missing People and the oddness of my experience with the London PI, the world of the searchers had begun to appear as diverse and complicated as the missing themselves. The more people I spoke with, the more perspectives I had to layer onto my own. There was no single professional scripture that spoke to and for the missing, that much was self-evident. Each individual, within their differing agencies and sectors, had their own specialisms and idiosyncrasies to add to or subtract from the whole. Whatever else separated them, the final goal was the same. The missing were out there and had to be found. You had to operate on the belief that the missing could be found.

From way back, right to my second cold cup of tea in the NCA offices in the summer of 2019, I'd started to think about hope. Not my own hoped-for resolution – which I hardly understood then – but instead for the dreams of others. At the end of that first conversation, after all the difficulties and enormous challenges inherent in the NCA's work, the tone started to brighten slightly. Joe believed that more people were becoming aware of the missing and their implications for the health of our society and pointed to the work going on in Scotland and elsewhere – the first few bits of tentative proof that something, anything, was starting to change to cope with the scale of the problem at hand. There was talk of all the effort that had gone into the still incomplete National Missing Persons Register, many long years in the making, and various other plans for the rest of the year.

Eventually we ran out of time and Joe had made his apologies, though we were certain this wasn't to be our last meeting. After being led again through the tangle of corridors and out of the front entrance, I made my way back to the tube through a sky of dark clouds that were hanging over that humid late afternoon. Vauxhall's Pleasure Gardens were almost entirely empty and silent, save for the dull thunder of traffic from the nearby main road. I couldn't see any sign of the tents or the men from earlier in that day and wondered if they'd found a better spot to rest as a thick rain started to fall and break the thickness of the clouds overhead. My time with the searchers had thrown open a thousand more questions, with many to be answered in good time. After making my way home, I sat down for a while at my laptop, trying to think about the next step on my journey through the maze of the disappeared. I knew then that it was time to take myself to the other place, down into the cracks where the missing themselves might have fallen.

PART III
THE PLACES YOU GO

CHAPTER 4

The threat of rain felt like something from another life, as I made my way across London on a freezing December morning. I'd woken early to unbroken blue skies, as I packed my bag for the day to come. From Elephant and Castle, I took the Northern Line all the way north to Chalk Farm. The tube was as quiet as the south London streets had been. I reasoned to myself that it was just luck, too soon in the day for the last-minute Christmas shoppers frantically making their way to central London, fuelled by guilt and adrenaline. Or maybe all of the non-Londoners had already made their way home, pouring out of the city on rammed tight trains from the major stations.

Whatever the reason, there was something in the air. The strange, almost lazy feeling of tranquillity that falls between Christmas week and New Year's Eve when the surface activity of the city is forced to slow and its offices shutter. It's always been my favourite time of year here. It was when, as a small child, my aunty and I would get the 185 bus up to St James's Park in the few days of dead time before New Year's Eve, and walk about aimlessly, enjoying one of London's silliest and most ornate parks free of the usual crush of tourists. It wasn't a memory at the forefront of my mind as I emerged blinking into the light at Chalk Farm and it took a few minutes to regain my bearings. North London isn't somewhere I know too well or visit all that often.

It felt like the day was opening up into itself as I walked the five or so minutes to Haverstock School. The comprehensive was Camden's first private finance initiative (PFI) rebuild back in 2006 and has the same cookie cutter, lightly managerial New Labour aesthetic of so many British schools built during the period: a world of glass facades and open-plan 'social areas'. It had just gone past 10 a.m. and it looked to be busy by the steps to the main entrance, even though the school's Christmas holidays had already begun a few days prior. The crowd was diverse. Men and women of all ages, some wearing lanyards and carrying clipboards, others taking their directions as they moved into the building. Inside the front doors, I was greeted by a couple of enthusiastic volunteers who pointed me to the press centre in the repurposed cafeteria on the ground floor.

The first morning of Crisis at Christmas was as busy as I'd been told it would be. Haverstock School was just one of their 15 centres spread out over London and the rest of the UK, from Coventry to Edinburgh. Its aims have remained the same since being established in 1972, alongside Crisis's year-round work: the provision of food, warmth and services for people facing homelessness over the festive period. The passing decades have seen the scale of the charity's seasonal operations grow, with over 11,000 dedicated volunteers working every year in the kitchens, or offering professional advice on access to benefits and healthcare, housing and work opportunities. More than 4,500 guests pass through their centres each festive period, some for temporary respite and a meal, others for its full duration, from 23 December to the evening of the 29th. After being handed a cup of tea, I was left with a cheerful young volunteer who took me on a whistle-stop tour of the building. As we dodged through the increasingly busy corridors she pointed out the neat rows of beds and an already packed kitchen, prepping for the days and nights to come.

It's estimated that over 320,000 people[4] are currently homeless in the UK, according to Shelter, another of the UK's largest and best-known homelessness and housing charities. For many, the thought of homelessness is directly equivalent to rough sleeping – by far its most visible form. It's not a foolish or inexplicable misconception. The same research shows that between 4,000 and 5,000 people bed down on the UK's streets every night, a figure that is almost double what it was in 2010, though like the numbers of missing, many believe the true figure to be far higher. The official numbers confirm what many have perceived with their eyes in towns and cities across the country. It doesn't matter so much where; London or Edinburgh, Cardiff or Manchester, things have visibly got worse all over. For some, it's only something noticed in increments, or after a period of absence. In 2018, a British friend of mine who had spent the previous few years living in Europe was shocked on arriving back in London to discover just how many more people she saw living out on the streets. Was this, she asked, just what things were like now?

It's not as simple as pointing to utopias elsewhere on the continent. The last decade has seen rates of homelessness climb across Europe. Ireland has seen rates of family homelessness explode, while in France the number of deaths in homeless shelters doubled between 2016 and 2019. While the German shelter system is considered to be one of the continent's best, with street homelessness relatively well managed, it's Finland that has made the biggest strides in the EU with its radical Housing First policy. Instead of the arcane 'staircase model' used by so many other European countries (the moving through stages of temporary accommodation on the way to permanent housing), the Finnish solution was simple: the unconditional offer of housing, no matter the individual's needs, as well as a sustained home-building programme backed with significant funding (including the conversion of a former shelter into a block of flats). Since its launch in 2008 homelessness in Finland has fallen by more than 35 per cent.

I'd first started to seriously consider homelessness as another strand of missing at the start of 2019, when my reporting led me to the work of Maeve McClenaghan, an award-winning investigative journalist with The Bureau of

Investigative Journalism, who worked on Dying Homeless, TBIJ's year-long campaign to chart the number of homeless deaths in the UK. Maeve started working on the project in early 2018, just after wrapping up a long investigation into domestic violence refuges, she'd told me over the phone. Both brought up questions around housing and vulnerable people. There were a slew of news reports honing in on a few particular deaths, including Marcos Amaral Gourgel outside the Houses of Parliament in February of 2018. That presented what she thought must be a simple question: if the number of homeless people had shot up in the years since 2009, then had the number of deaths related to home-lessness risen alongside? The answer ended up being a lot more complicated than Maeve, or anyone else, had initially thought. At first, no one could give a straight answer. The coroner's office would ask her to try the police, who would tell her to try the council, who would pass her on to the coroner's office. The looping round continued, until it suddenly dawned on her that no one knew because nobody had bothered to keep count. 'There has been a consistent degradation of the safety net,' Maeve explained to me when we spoke on the phone in early 2019. 'People have to be in an absolute crisis before they access mental health services, though I was speaking to a woman who has been in acute crises and couldn't get the support she needed. The lack of social housing is of course an issue, but so is the massive increase in private rents, while housing benefit has stayed low.'

The Bureau spoke with homelessness charities and organisations, journalists, healthcare professionals and people
from all over the country, and uncovered many half-forgotten tragedies. The 51-year-old man who had killed himself
the day before his temporary accommodation ran out, a
grandmother found dead in a car park and a man who was
tipped into a bin lorry while he slept; 449 deaths in 12
months, a rate of more than one a day. The message of the
state's inertia seemed clear enough: some lives, and deaths,
deserve more dignity than others.

How had it come to this? In the Crisis cafeteria, I sat
down to talk with David, a softly spoken white-haired man
with a Scottish accent in his early 60s. He told me that he
wasn't a guest this year, but had been in 2018, one of the
most difficult years of his life, when he had returned to the
UK after 25 years living and teaching academic English in
Japan. It seemed a clear enough process, that as a UK citizen and passport holder he would be able to return and
start to build the next chapter of his life. He suffered few
illusions about what it might hold, as a single man at his
age taking such a profound step. Like so many big decisions, it wasn't taken in haste or with the expectation of
uninterrupted bliss at the end of it. But David couldn't have
predicted just how wrong things would get, or how quickly.
'I came back thinking that within a month to six weeks, I'd
be teaching again. I had my passport and perhaps naively
thought it would be that simple. As it turned out, that
wasn't sufficient these days,' he explained to me carefully

through slightly pursed lips, as if the recollection still caused him physical pain. 'In a sense I was almost quasi-stateless. I'm not blaming individuals within government organisations or local authorities. But it took me seven and a half months to get my National Insurance number, which had been lost somewhere along the line. [Perhaps] bureaucracies are slow wherever you are. They aren't designed for individuals. If you exist outside of one of their criteria, they can't cope.'

Without either an NI number or his NHS number, David found himself essentially locked out from the essentials of an even halfway tolerable life and there was nothing he could do about it. The new start had quickly turned into a nightmare as his small savings evaporated and soon enough David found himself facing homelessness. And what would happen if his health started to suffer? He was, after all, not a young man anymore. 'Without either of those numbers, I couldn't work, I couldn't rent, I couldn't open a bank account. It led me to sofa surfing and a few nights – not too many thank God – of sleeping rough. [Eventually] I was picked up by Ealing Churches, who referred me on to Crisis and it's because of them that I ended up here last year. It was wonderful. I got medical attention and a haircut, as well as advice and support. It was a safe place to stay and they worked with me [to find a permanent housing solution].' After months in limbo, around midway through 2019, David's NI number was finally located. He could rejoin the systems that needed to be rejoined and begin to start thinking about somewhere to settle down. After some deliberation, it seemed like Birmingham might be the right fit. 'I had looked at a couple of places in London but it's so exorbitantly expensive and the difference between what you pay and what you're getting is so pronounced. [Birmingham] was actually suggested to me by my support worker at Crisis and also by a housing officer in Ealing.' Though it wasn't a city David knew first-hand, it carried at least some familiarity. 'Some of my students in Japan were actually preparing to take their master's in the city, though most are in London of course. I knew that it's a major educational hub, so that made sense. I have a smashing studio flat and we're working on getting me into a housing association or council flat. I just hope once that's sorted I can start teaching again,' he added with the thin hint of a smile on his face. Had he considered himself missing at any point throughout his ordeal, I'd wondered. It wasn't an easy question to ask or answer. The difference in the life he'd thought he'd be returning to and the one that awaited him was vast. If anything, it was the vision he had for his own future that had started to disappear, as he rapidly started to fall from sight.

Though David's story ended on a cautiously hopeful note, and though he'd said he didn't feel any rancour towards the individuals that represented the state bodies that had denied him the means to live, it didn't mean he wasn't angry at the existence of a system that caused such misery, for so many. 'I don't know how folk cope,' he added quietly. 'This is the twenty-first century. It's beyond appalling that this kind of situation is even conceivable.' Before arriving back in the UK after his many years of absence, David didn't know that things in his life would slip like this, or even perhaps that they could. In Japan he had been a visible member of society, with a respectable job and a home. With structure and dignity. These were not small things and he knew that there would be some risk in returning from the life he had built for himself and coming back to the land of his birth. In the UK, he was just a single man, without family or an extended network. The friends he did have, he soon had to rely on. For someone who had been self-reliant for so long, it didn't feel natural, or anything like himself. 'The sofa surfing exhausts the patience of friends,' as David put it succinctly. 'They have their own things going on too.' And if it could be like this for him, what was it like out there for others? The old cliché has it that most of us are only a couple of missed pay cheques away from homelessness, but some are more vulnerable than others. One recent report by Shelter found that homelessness had risen by 9 per cent for white households between 2012 and 2017. For BAME households that figure was 48 per cent. As homeownership rates have fallen across the board, the drop has been steeper among black and Asian households, who often face discrimination from private landlords. And according to LGBTQ+ homelessness charity Akt, a quarter of all homeless young people in the UK identify as LGBT; the majority pointing to strained relationships with their parents after coming out as the main cause of their predicament. Burrowing down into the figures painted an alarming picture, a nationwide crisis that disproportionately impacts on the poorest and most marginalised.

After talking with David, it was clear that the centre was starting to fill up. Any vestige of early-morning tranquillity was starting to fade, as lunchtime approached. Before long, I got talking to Lucy, a cheerful woman in her mid-20s. She'd been talking about herself most of the morning, she laughed, though she didn't mind explaining her story to me again. Growing up, she and her younger brother had lived in an abusive household with their mother. For years, the siblings had flitted in and out of care, never quite sticking around anywhere long enough to properly consider it home. When Lucy was 19, she went to live with her mother again during her last year of A levels. It didn't last for long. 'She was really abusive again and ended up chucking me out of the house. That's when I got into sofa surfing, effectively,' Lucy told me. 'The first night I ended up going to stay with my friend and staying for a few days. It didn't last either as there wasn't much room. I didn't know where to go or what to do.' The last few years have witnessed a growing awareness of sofa surfing as a particularly insidious form of hidden homelessness, just another way of falling out of view. At the end of 2019, research conducted by Crisis[5] revealed the contemporary scale of an issue that has rarely before received serious scrutiny. Their work found that of the 170,000 'core homeless households' –

those experiencing rough sleeping, night shelters or unsuitable temporary accommodation – more than 71,000 are thought to be sofa surfing. Like Lucy and David, it means depending on the sometimes brittle kindness of friends, family and acquaintances, often for protracted periods of time. Though the term itself sounds almost benign, there's nothing soft about its strains and privations. The first night wasn't easy for Lucy, but things would only get harder as the weeks dragged on. 'It was around six months overall that I was sofa surfing, so I'd say I lived in quite a few people's houses over that time. Of course, I didn't want to be a burden. The problem is though, you're always a burden. You're always that little bit on edge. Some of my friendships were permanently strained because of it and it's upsetting. It's horrible that either of you has to be put in that position, but it's unavoidable really, in that situation.' Eventually, one of Lucy's teachers found out about her predicament. 'I'd been looking at accommodation through the YMCA, but it was a months-long application process. Through one of her friends, I ended up finding a spare room. There was also the matter of not being able to source housing benefit before, as I didn't have an address. Without a stable place you can't make a claim.' Like David, she had been caught between the gaps of a system that seemed incapable of dealing with the intricacies of individual lives, rather than pre-programmed templates. That fortunate shot at stability led to the start of a new life for Lucy. She isn't hidden anymore. From A levels to an undergraduate degree, she's currently working towards a PhD in social care at Oxford and living in a stable housing situation.

The outline of Lucy's tale made me think about Mum and Christobal, when they'd first arrived together in London. In the years and months before my birth, they'd flitted from flat to flat, sofa to sofa, spare bed to spare bed, with each sanctuary as temporary as the last. It was nothing to do with a lack of will from them or of empathy from their loved ones. Instead, it was all about the everyday and familiar consequences of poverty, of never having quite enough to bundle together and put down on a place to call your own. When I was born, it meant the flat in Hither Green. This was still a city where the prospect of a council flat wasn't something fantastical. It hadn't become a myth yet, something fit for only the wildest dreams. The latest figures show 10,000 people on the Lewisham Council waiting list and more than 2,000 families stuck in temporary accommodation in the borough. If I had been born now instead of then would Mum and Christobal have waited, through more months and years of uncertainty in the city? There's no way of saying that they would have, or if they'd have decided enough was enough, that it was time to leave London and their networks of friends and family, their employment and all either of them had ever known in the country. In the end, it was a dilemma that was solved with the offer of a one-bedroom flat. For the tens of thousands of families facing that choice in the capital today, it is an ending that will never be an option.

For some observers, it's easy to shrug and say that it doesn't sound all that difficult, that surely people deal with worse every day. It's the kind of bluff-sounding common sense that comes from people who have never had to uproot their lives, or experience any upheaval they haven't chosen for themselves. In 2017, it came to light that a handful of London councils were making aggressive use of legal powers to make what reporters at the *Guardian*[6] termed 'take it or leave it offers' of housing far away from the city, in a bid to resettle hundreds of legally homeless families. The process was as blunt as its name suggested, with families given 24 hours to decide whether to accept homes in Essex, the West Midlands or other parts of the South East, some more than 100 miles away from London. If declined, the council would immediately start to consider them 'intentionally homeless' and wash their hands of any further responsibility. In one case outlined in the same article, 'Brent council offered a three-bedroomed private rented property in Telford, Shropshire to 11 homeless families over a 12-month period. All refused or were deemed to have refused the property without seeing it. Nine of the families had jobs in the capital, and all had at least two children in local schools.' It begs the question: why should people be forced out of the lives they've built? Of course, the slow death of the UK's truly affordable housing is by no means just about London. The last few decades have seen its rapid erosion, all over the UK. What used to be a fact barely worth remarking on is now a vanishing rarity. The construction of social housing has dropped by 80 per cent over the past decade, with almost a million people on waiting lists, forced into precarious private rentals that often take up half their earnings or more. Just another kind of absence. The vanishing of the opportunity to build a dignified life in stable housing.

CHAPTER 5

It was a different kind of winter morning as I made my way to Manchester at the end of January 2020, just over a month from my visit to Crisis at Christmas. There was something heavy in the air as I left home and made my way to Euston for the 10 a.m. train north. The station was packed at the back end of rush hour, so I stood back against the wall, craning my neck to the electronic departures board to check which platform I'd need to dash to. The two and a bit hours went smoothly enough, on a far quieter carriage than I'd been expecting. Two middle-aged women on the seats behind me chatted amiably the whole journey, mainly about their respective sons and their respective mortgages, with a few interludes of office gossip thrown in for the sake of variety. This snapshot into their lives was soothing; small eavesdropped dramas that required no context or after-thought. It had been a busy start to the year and I was already beginning to feel it. The chance to sit back, even for a couple of hours, was a welcome change from my routine of reporting around London during the short days and long nights. Soon enough though, the fields had given way to the seemingly endless suburbs, which finally blurred into the city proper and the noise and bustle of Piccadilly station.

I was there to meet Hendrix Lancaster for the first time, CEO of local homelessness charity Coffee4Craig. It felt like a long time coming, the invite to pay them a visit in their city-centre offices arriving after months of emails back and forth. They are always busy, in a city where the number of registered rough sleepers rose from seven in 2010 to 123 by 2018.[7] The charity was started in the aftermath of a personal tragedy for Hendrix and his wife and fellow co-founder Risha Lancaster. In September 2013, Risha's brother, Craig White, was found dead after a heroin overdose, where he had been living on the streets after a relationship had broken down. Craig was just 37 when he died alone in a car park in Cardiff city centre. How had it ended like this, so quickly? There are many more like Craig all over the UK, living lives that start to slip for whatever reason, where it just takes a few steps before a chasm starts to open up beneath them. Though Craig died alone, he hasn't been forgotten. The charity started life the same month as his passing, with the family wanting to do something, anything, to alleviate the suffering they could see every day in Manchester city centre. (Manchester is a city particularly marked by the missing. The most recent figures published by the NCA's Missing Persons Unit[8] showed how Greater Manchester Police dealt with more people going missing unexpectedly than any other force in the country, relative to population size in 2018–19. Of the 31,805 missing incidents, over half were children and 243 were classed as long-term missing, their whereabouts still unknown.) They took things small at the start. Hendrix and Risha began to hand out coffees, with the message that 'this is from Craig'. It didn't take long to progress past hot drinks, as their band of well-wishers and volunteers began to grow. By the end of 2013, they were running an outdoor street kitchen, three nights a week in Piccadilly Gardens, a decently sized shock of green space in the middle of Manchester city centre. As the years have passed, the scale of their operation has continued to grow along with the rough sleeping numbers in the city. In 2016, they entered into a partnership with Centrepoint, one of the country's best known homelessness charities, a relationship that turned the three-night kitchen into a seven-day-a-week drop-in centre along with two other local organisations. More than anything else, the centre operates as somewhere to be seen for those who use its services. A sanctuary for the men and women the charity tends to, a place for a hot shower, a square meal and some temporary respite from the chaos of life on the streets.

Having arrived an hour early, I took the chance to walk through the city centre, letting my feet carry me around in unfamiliar patterns from Manchester Art Gallery to King Street and the Coffee4Craig office. The wind was up and the streets mainly quiet. It felt like what it was, another blurred midwinter working day, the kind that isn't readymade for excitement or epiphanies. All I could think about was the cold on my skin as I finally arrived at the right building. Having settled down, I sat on a sofa in the lobby of what looked like a cheerful co-working space for various different companies, full of bustling and trendy-looking young people who could have been working at anything at all, from new media start-up to graphic design agency. Before long, Hendrix joined me with a firm handshake, alongside Hannah, one of the charity's key support workers. I put the two of them in their early 30s, with both immediately giving the impression of people who lived their jobs intensely. It was, as always, a pretty frantic time, with a long-planned-for office move on the horizon and a million and one other immediate concerns to attend to, every other moment of the day. Not that there's ever really a 'typical day' in their line of work, Hannah explained. 'The only thing that stays the same is how different it is every day. Someone new will walk in with such a different story. There are also plenty who return, a lot of the same guys [but it can be] sad how much has changed since I started four years ago. And I'll never not be shocked at some of what we see and I'm never prepared for how much it can change, so quickly.' For Hendrix, it's an important reaction to retain in a working world where so many suffer from burnout at the scale and relentlessness of the task in hand. 'It's a good thing,' he replied, 'that none of us have lost our shock factor – none of us have lost that real empathy and desire to make just one person's life better each day. That for me is everything.'

Some of the faces that pass through their doors are fresh to the streets. These are the people that might have gone through their first or second night of rough sleeping. The particularly vulnerable who would get eaten alive arriving at shelters where conditions can be cramped and fraught, or some of the temporary accommodation in the city. They haven't yet developed the experience to cope with their new reality, with everything still a blur, stuck at a point perilously close to missing. 'They're one of the two extremes,' Hendrix added. 'There are those just hitting the streets who haven't experienced anything like it in their lives, right up to the most chaotic individuals who have been out there for years. Those who have been in and out of the system, trapped in a constantly revolving door. The challenge for them both is finding the right accommodation.'

For many arriving for help, their lives are marked by other issues that can make that challenge feel daunting. Mental health crops up regularly in our conversation. 'It can be that their issues are too severe to access certain shelters and accommodation but not severe enough to be put under a section. So they're in that middle ground, but aside from ringing the police and flagging up welfare with concerns there's not really a lot you can do, because nobody will take them,' Hendrix added. It can be a source of intense frustration, to put it mildly. The question of capacity is a difficult one, with different answers dependent on who exactly it is you're asking. Who decides exactly where the line is, for an individual's ability to make rational choices about their own welfare? Paramedics and healthcare workers will look to see if people can retain and repeat information, though police have a different criteria, as do social services, who work by the 2014 Care Assessment Act. 'It should be standardised,' Hendrix told me. For Hannah, it's scary, there's no other way of putting it. More and more people every year are coming through the door, with less and less grasp of where they are. '[We see] people when you think, "How can this person be considered to have the capacity to make decisions?" You're looking at them and they're dying. They're dying in front of you.' It isn't hyperbole. Things can get as bad as that and often do. They have seen people with ulcerated legs, on the verge of sepsis. 'Our medic is basically keeping them alive day to day, but they won't go to hospital, they won't access any further kind of medical care. How can you say that person has capacity? The limit of their capacity is "I want to take drugs", and that is it. The fact that their leg is potentially going to be amputated [doesn't seem] to come into it,' Hendrix added with increasing animation.

The drug trade is not a new concern for Manchester's homeless population. Life for the city's street users is marked by many of the usual substances, mainly heroin and crack, but they aren't what Manchester has become synonymous with over the last half decade and more. Spice first appeared on the scene in the early 2010s, as the most popular of what were christened 'legal highs'. Marketed as synthetic cannabis, it was – and is – easy and cheap enough to get hold of, from shops and vendors all across the city, just as it was all over the country before its 2016 ban, under the Psychoactive Substances Act. The first astonished reports noticed what it would do to people. 'It hits you like a train,' one former user told me. 'One second you're there, the next is like … it's like nothing else.' It can be a frightening thing to witness. Seizures are commonplace, twisting people up into 'zombie-like' states for prolonged periods of time. The ban didn't do much to stem its rise in Manchester, far from it. Street dealing is rife and open, right in the city centre. Piccadilly Gardens is a particular hotspot, though the harm has also transferred out to the city's suburbs and satellite towns. Enterprising dealers can head into town, pick up a gram for £5 and head back out to sell it for triple the price in suburbia.

Like anything else, it can ebb and flow, though there doesn't seem to be much predictability or pattern. Between 2015 and 2018, things were particularly dark: batches and strains kept getting stronger and knocking even experienced users over the edge. Hannah told how there was a point when ambulances were getting called out every five to ten minutes. 'What happens is the car will roll up [and] drop off a bag of McDonald's wrappers out of the passenger window. Someone would pick it up and you'd see all the [drug dealers'] runners sitting around with their man-bags and that. Then these 14- to 17-year-old lads just disperse and then within five minutes you see all the guys on the streets just collapsing, foaming at the mouth, throwing up

– we had a couple of guys bleeding out of their mouth and nose.' The night before my visit they'd had to deal with an older guy, not a regular spice user, who'd picked up a cigarette end from the floor. After one toke, he'd turned white and collapsed, having not long recovered from heart surgery. Thankfully, he survived. It doesn't help that things in the drug trade are liable to change perpetually. When we spoke it was street opiates that were starting to cause trouble, a sudden surge of cheap and potent benzos (benzodiazepines, the family of drugs that Valium comes from). All the homelessness services had been feeling it, Hendrix added. 'The police said [they'd] been taken from one of these pharmaceutical storage units near Trafford. We were seeing it everywhere, we were finding blister packs everywhere.'

Hendrix and Hannah, just like Joe and Kirsty from Missing People, are not individuals to live in despair. They are under no illusions of 'solving' homelessness in Manchester. The problems are many and they are interlinked. Like the missing, there is no spell to cast to bring the lost and damaged back into vision. But that is no reason for nihilism. The issues are there, to be tackled: there are people there, to be helped. There are so many good things that come with their work. For some of those they work with, they are the closest thing to family. Recently, they managed to help a long-term client of theirs into a secure flat, after years of being on the streets. 'He's just got keys and is so overwhelmed by it,' Hannah explained. Though he's in recovery, it's early days. Three months to be exact. 'He did a two-week detox and we'd been battling to keep him in some sort of accommodation until the flat was ready. If [he'd gone] straight back on the streets there was a big chance of him relapsing.' The big move-in day was imminent, Hendrix added. 'He used to be bouncing off the walls, couldn't get a proper sentence out of him. If I ever saw him on the streets and asked him if he'd like to drop in for a chat he'd say, "Nope, going to score." He probably gets about fifty hours a week solid support just from us. It's a gap that needs filling, and that's cool, that's what we do – we fill gaps.'

Like many other similar charities up and down the UK, their work is akin to an adhesive, spread across a crumbling support system, an edifice deeply pockmarked and cracked. Coffee4Craig run the only late-night referral route for emergency shelter in the entire city, with a population of over half a million. It takes a moment for that to sink in. That's for all of Manchester, I asked again, still slightly taken aback. 'Yeah,' Hendrix replied, 'during the day there's [other] centres, the town hall, etc., but they close at 4 p.m. Then from 6 to 9 p.m. there's an out-of-hours service, and from 9 p.m. until 2/3 a.m. Risha and I and our volunteers take over and do the night-time referral routes. [On one occasion] we managed to get 30 individuals into bed spaces. That was pretty successful.' Services are stretched in the city, though that hardly makes it unique in the UK after the decade of cuts and enforced austerity of the 2010s. Winter is the hardest time of year and it feels like it's getting longer every year. Even though it was January, neither Hendrix nor Hannah believed anything like the worst of the weather had hit yet. A couple of years before, Hendrix told me, the cold winter season lasted from November to April. 'All those nights,' he explained, '[were] a killer.' As the light fades and temperatures plummets, people can get desperate. But things seemed to be on the up from a low ebb, with both Hendrix and Hannah talking positively about Manchester's mayor, Labour stalwart Andy Burnham, who seemed to be taking homelessness with a genuine serious-ness that went beyond his immediate predecessors. As our meeting ran to a close, we set a tentative time to meet again, before I let them go and get on with their work, grateful for the hours they'd already given me. Before my train home, I took a walk down to Piccadilly Gardens, to watch the commotion and bustle of another afternoon. It was rush hour again, as I sat down at my window seat, hurtling back home at the same time Coffee4Craig would be getting ready for another night and all the people it would bring through their doors.

CHAPTER 6

My thoughts were with Hendrix and Hannah in the weeks before the UK inched into lockdown, in March 2020. Though barely three months had passed, it felt like decades had elapsed from the world that permitted carefree train travel and reporting day trips between cities. The weeks where the old certainties started to crumble into chaos. One of the most striking developments was the government's announcement of Everyone In, an ambitious scheme to temporarily house all of the UK's rough sleepers, to shield them as the pandemic spread, in empty hotels and hostels across the country. But questions immediately presented themselves. Why had it taken extraordinary circumstances to solve a problem everyone knew about and had been warning against for years? Some pointed to the fact that the scheme at least had the benefit of decisiveness. In some quarters, it was portrayed as an unequivocal success, with the government's figures showing that local authorities had housed more than 14,000 people[9] in England alone, even if the true number might have been just a third of that, according to sceptical experts who quickly made their voices known. For many who benefited, the scheme was no small thing: it offered the chance of somewhere stable to sleep and a square meal, as well as access to services under the same roof. So it seemed inconceivable when news started to filter through that rough sleeping had actually increased at the same time its temporary eradication was being trumpeted. Figures from Streetlink, a service that connects rough sleepers with local outreach teams in England and Wales, showed just as much. Between April and June 2020, the service saw 16,976 'alerts' recorded, a 4 per cent rise from January to March and a 36 per cent increase from 2019.[10] In London, those figures had been even more pronounced, with 4,277 people sleeping rough between April and June 2020, two-thirds of whom were doing so for the first time, a 77 per cent rise from the same period in 2019.[11]

It seemed that despite the government's misleading numbers, the scale of the crisis was as severe as ever. In June, I'd spoken with Nail Parkinson, joint head of casework at Glass Door, a London-based homelessness charity who had been swamped during the lockdown months. Similarly to Coffee4Craig, they are there to plug the gaps in the system and respond to the needs of those that come in the door, whatever they may be. They don't carry out assessments or referrals for their shelters and never have done. 'We don't check for ID or anything like that. The ethos is meeting the need and then building up trust and eventually resolving their homelessness, which is where the casework service comes in,' Neil explained. 'We try to maintain that balance and acknowledge people have complex issues that might take time to resolve. People can stay up to two years in our shelters, though we do make exceptions.' The charity don't actually run any day centres directly, but are partnered with half a dozen across west and south-west London. 'There's Richmond, Clapham, Chelsea, South Kensington, Earls Court and Hammersmith. Our case workers are based out of there. We work with CHAIN [Combined Homelessness and Information Network – the multi-agency database with the names of London's recorded rough sleepers] and think about 50 per cent of our guests are CHAIN verified, while 50 per cent aren't. That shows how wide the problem is beyond the verified rough sleeping population.' The other half are invisible, hidden from sight, somewhere beyond the statistics – a number they could already see climbing in 2020 as people struggled with a new kind of precarity occasioned by the pandemic. Just as the 180,000 reported missing is only an estimate, the numbers recorded by GlassDoor only spoke to a fraction of the true homelessness figures. '[The rest] might be sofa surfing, they might be in parks or buses, or just never showing up in any system,' Neil continued. 'We try to act as a bit of a one-stop shop. Housing is our ultimate goal, but we understand that a lot of things feed into that. [Things like] benefits and employment, for example.'

I read over my notes from my talk with Neil on the train up the east coast for a couple of days alone in Newcastle later that summer, in the first week of August 2020. It was my first visit to the Tyneside city, on my way up to Dundee. Though it hadn't been planned as an aimless solo ramble, that's what it had quickly become after two people I was due to interview had to cancel at the last minute. Having already booked the train and an aggressively functional Airbnb, I decided there were worse places for a few moody walks and bouts of morbid self-reflection in high summer.

In truth, North East England has always been a bit of a mystery to me. For years, there had never really been any reason to visit, no friends or family to call on. If not now, I'd reasoned, when would it ever happen? I've never needed much of an excuse to put things off. Sometime in my mid-20s I accepted that I might just be one of life's natural homebirds, happy enough to mill about in the familiarity of a few places that I knew well enough to lay roots in. It's not that I don't like to travel, or that I don't do quite a bit of it for work or pleasure, but there's a definite limit to the length of time I enjoy being away without starting to pine for the acquired taste and charms of suburban south-east London. Unlike Mum or Christobal, I've never really been all that close in my adult life to fully transplanting myself from my comfort zone, somewhere totally unfamiliar and strange. It might just be one of those things that either does or doesn't run in your blood, the kind of determined wanderlust that makes people forget the reasons why they shouldn't just launch themselves into the possibilities of life somewhere new, beyond the constraints of wherever they've happened to call home. I've always needed a focus for any trip: a family friend long overdue a dutiful visit, or some other appeal to the conscience. It's not that I refuse to be spontaneous, but I'm not quite sure it's ever really suited me, or come naturally. Not every parental trait can be transfigured into a straightforward inheritance. I've occasionally considered that my rootedness might be its own mild form of rejection of the kinds of lives my parents led and the choices they made – a small and inconsequential rejoinder to the idea that the present is entirely bound to the past. So it felt strange to still be hurtling north after my interviewees had politely rescheduled, on my way to a city I knew next to nothing about. Though maybe that isn't quite true. Over the past few years, I'd gained a growing number of friends who had studied or grown up in Newcastle, with some others who had just sort of landed there, for reasons ranging from partners to work. They'd mostly said variations of the same thing – what an unshowily fantastic city it was, full of good pubs and even better people, the sort of place that inspires strong feelings and a territorial sense of well-justified civic pride.

The recommendations started to pour in as soon as I'd put up a photo of the city centre on Instagram, a carefully curated list of places I had to visit, or eat and drink in. Naturally, after drawing up an earnest, almost militarily precise itinerary, I ended up no further than the first pub I recognised from the lists I'd been sent. The Tyne Bar was about 20 minutes from the off-season student halls I'd checked into, earlier that same overcast Sunday afternoon. Walking lazily down the waterfront, I let myself drift into a trance, smiling indulgently at the sight of young couples and cheerful families, walking at the same relaxed pace as myself. For a while, I just stood at the edge of the water, taking in the suspension bridges and converted factories along the Quayside as the sun started to break through the clouds, smugly convinced that I'd stumbled into the city at its most picturesque.

The pub was what various friends had promised, a solid little waterside spot with plenty of outdoor seating and enough space to avoid the more boisterous drinkers who didn't fit into my fairly half-hearted flâneur cosplay. Sipping at a pint, it would be untrue to say I had anything profound swirling around my skull, apart from a pleasant feeling of temporary, self-regulated loneliness: the kind of spell easily broken by a few texts dashed off to friends and family a few hundred miles away. The sky was dipping into night by the time I left, a swirl of ridiculous colour pressed firmly against a quickening darkness. And so the two days passed in Newcastle, a fog of undirected exploring and cheerful enough isolation.

It felt good to be alone after the lockdown months, though it didn't stop a few pathetic pangs of self-pity on the first night away from my partner, surely not helped by either the lager or the powerful burst of regression bound into finding yourself sleeping in student halls for the first time in almost a decade. Loneliness is like any other habit,

I suppose. It becomes easier with practice, whatever your natural temperament. It was something I was starting to consider ever more frequently, after my many months living with the spectre of the missing. For the lucky, like myself, it had only ever been a choice, taken to the point when being alone is a pleasure, to be sought after. The blessing and curse of the only child. For so many others, isolation is the backdrop of their entire lives. In Newcastle, I let my feet drift wherever they wanted to, safe in the knowledge that home was somewhere else, accessible, if just out of vision. I wondered if Christobal had ever been here, or Mum for that matter? But I doubt anyone remembers now. It's just another thing that no one has an answer to.

The new city wasn't an escape from the missing. I knew I had to come back at some point to meet my sources and there were reminders of work everywhere, just as there were in city centres I'd been visiting all over the country. Dotted around Newcastle, I'd come across the usual Missing People posters, with Andrew Gosden's face set against the appeal for donations and information. On my second afternoon of walking, I pulled out my notebook and jotted down the details on a notice for Street Zero, a charity set up to eradicate rough sleeping in the city by 2022. I'd long ago begun to suffer the side effects of my obsession with the missing and everything that sprang out of my searching for them, where everywhere you turn is another rabbit hole to be explored. Here I was in a brand new city, with nothing else to do than enjoy it and gather my thoughts for the months ahead, and still my brain couldn't help but point to more leads and causes to chase down.

It was a close, muggy morning as I boarded an almost deserted train to Dundee, cradling a coffee and a hastily grabbed banana from the Sainsbury's in the station. So far so normal, I thought to myself, despite the newly ubiquitous addition of a compulsory face mask. The journey was a leisurely three hours north, passing through a litany of unfamiliar towns and a few sudden bursts of dramatic coastal scenery. Precisely the sort of travel to finish some worthy reading or catch up on whatever big banner podcast you've been avoiding in your normal life. Instead, I just kept my eyes glued to the window looking out, quite enjoying the silence and the luxury of an entire carriage to myself. My solo ambling around Newcastle had given me a taste for idle contemplation and that's how I chose to pass the few hours until I arrived somewhere far more familiar.

Between 2010 and 2014, I lived and studied in Dundee. They were broadly happy, sometimes fraught years spent working towards a degree in English Literature. The city hadn't been my first choice and I'd ended up in Dundee pretty by default back then, having fouled up my exams at school. Looking back to that point in my life feels almost as far away as my memories of Christobal and Mum. It's a version of myself that feels as good as dead now. The unconvincingly cocky late adolescent with an absurd mop of hair and clothes that still had a faint trace of the disastrous late indie era: a tragic muddle of skinny jeans and cheap athleisure.

I can't remember how much I really knew about Dundee before my aunty dropped me off there on a balmy late morning that September, but it was fairly close to zero. My first impressions of the city were almost comically vivid, as I settled down to unpack my shoddily packed boxes of books and the few bits of practical homeware I'd managed to pick up in IKEA the week before. My new room was on the first floor of a rotting concrete tower that I was convinced had been airlifted from a former Soviet provincial city after a couple of decades' worth of neglect. Dundee was a different place then. Though nowhere stays entirely the same over the course of a decade, the rate of change has been pronounced. The latter half of the twentieth century had not been kind to Scotland's fourth largest city. Back when I'd first arrived, the centre was an impenetrable maze of interlocking roundabouts, crazily built concrete islands and the looming presence of Tayside House, a 1960s office block that looked like it had been slashed by a straight razor every time it rained, which it happened to do quite a lot of the time. For many, Dundee is a hard place to live, on a level quite beyond the architectural vandalism committed by its former council leaders. Child poverty rates are some of the highest in the UK and the second highest in Scotland, with 31 per cent of children in the city living in families desperately struggling to make ends meet.[12] The gaps are ever widening, between those at the harshest end and those living in middle-class comfort. While the centre of the old industrial area of Lochee is the 20th most deprived ward in the entire country, the nearby West End is one of the most affluent: a difference that calculates to very different health outcomes and life expectancies. In 2018, Dundee attracted unwelcome headlines proclaiming it the drug death capital of Europe,[13] an inaccurate moniker that only piled further stigma on the city (EU countries record stats differently, making comparisons meaningless). But that isn't to deny the scale of the problem. Over the past decade more than 400 people have died drug-related deaths in the city. In 2018, there were over a thousand in Scotland, with Dundee accounting for 53[14] of those – the highest of any area in the country. Heroin has been a long-term problem, but it's 'street Valium' (the same cheap, potent opiates circulating in Manchester) that have proved particularly deadly. It's a toxic cocktail. Slashed services, poverty and a flood of deadly drugs bought with incredible levels of ease from street dealers all around the city. Dundee is a small place, the kind of city where everyone knows everyone. It doesn't take long to find those living with the memory of someone lost to what has taken on the severity of a public health crisis. So many gone and so many lost.

But Dundee isn't just the sum of its struggles. It's also a lively place, without any pretension. Despite the clichés tagged on to its reputation, it can often be a beautiful city, full of handsome tenements and the constant surprise of the river, rearing into view at unexpected angles. The autumn of 2018 also saw the opening of the long-anticipated V&A Dundee, after several delays and an ever spiralling budget running into the hundreds of millions. It was to be the frontispiece of an ambitious process of arts-led regeneration, dispensing with the mistakes of the past and burrowing forward into a brave, if still vaguely, defined new future. I got to see it myself just a few weeks after the grand opening, on one of my sporadic visits up for work. I'd been reporting on a long feature about the spike in drug-related deaths and had spent a few days on my own, retracing my old stomping grounds and interviewing a mixture of charities, frontline workers and people struggling with homelessness and addiction. It was the first time I'd visited Eagles Wings Trust, a small Christian charity with a space up on Douglas Street, one line of a maze of post-industrial lanes, streets and byways about 15 minutes' walk from the gleaming new waterfront. For the last decade they've worked to support those living in the shadow of addiction, often in precarious housing situations. Things are different in Dundee. It isn't London or Manchester, or even Newcastle. Street homelessness is less of an immediately pressing concern here, though it is never quite in danger of being eradicated entirely. Affordable housing is still a possibility, though it still isn't always easy to access it, for those most in need.

Eagles Wings Trust are right on the frontline, working with some of the city's most vulnerable and marginalised, day after day at their drop-in centre, night after night at their city-centre soup kitchen. It was there, in the autumn of 2018, that I first met Jason (not his real name, which he didn't want used), a 25-year-old with a mop of brown hair and cautious eyes. We got talking over a cup of tea, though he was wary about offering up too much. After some small talk, we settled on a plan to meet over the next couple of days, at the drop-in. It didn't need any special perceptiveness to realise he was nervous, in the natural manner of someone unused to explaining the tangle of his life out loud. Originally from the outskirts of Edinburgh, he had moved to Dundee a number of years before to be with his partner at the time. For a while, things were ok in his new life on the east coast. His upbringing hadn't been the happiest, there were problems at home and he'd never really got on too well with his immediate family. So the new start felt good, just him, his partner and their young child.

Things started to change sometime in the early 2010s. He'd started on the legal highs, back before they were banned in 2016 – though he told me he wasn't using benzos, even if many of his friends were. Spice and its various different strains were readily available everywhere you went back then. In fact, there was a shop in a dingy arcade in the city centre that could sort out all of your needs, for far less than the 20 quid it would set you back for a couple of grams of weed.

'That was it,' Jason had said. 'That's all it took for things to get out of control.'

When things were at their worst, using was an everyday occurrence. 'I was spending all my money and just like going away for days at a time back then.' Of course, his loved ones were worried and so was he, as the weeks blurred into months. It was like hell, he explained. He wasn't himself, or anyone he even dimly recognised. His head wasn't right and the days kept slipping out of control. The drugs took over his attention and were soon taking over his life. And where was he when he went missing on his benders? 'Do you believe in addiction?' he'd asked me about halfway into our chat as the sun started to stream through the windows. Yes, I'd answered back, I believe in addiction, having been exposed to some of Christobal's problems in my early years. My talk with Jason reminded me of him, long before this book was even a coherent idea. Their shared frailty and sense of not quite belonging in the worlds they'd found themselves living in. And what about Jason's family, I wanted to know. Though he was in recovery, it had only followed after an estrangement from his former partner and young boys. At the darkest moments he thought about death. His family back on the east coast didn't try to understand his predicament, or didn't want to. Lonely. That's what he was. That's what he felt like all the time. Since 2018, Jason has been in recovery, with Eagles Wings Trust a big part of his development. It is a fragile state, but he was making progress. The charity, just like Coffee4Craig in Manchester, is a place to go and be seen and accepted, a place where people at least understand what it means to have been in dependency and can help with pointing you in the right direction for treatment and whatever services are available. It stopped him from falling out of vision entirely.

The present was hard and the future uncertain but at least there were now a few opportunities to see his sons. 'I don't want them to live like I have. That just can't happen [so I need] to carry on going,' he'd added. Perhaps naively, I asked if there was anywhere else he could go to break away from the pressures in Dundee, of old friends and habits that could draw him back into the things he'd worked so hard to climb clear from. But where would he go? 'I can't go back [and] there isn't another place I can probably afford, so [this] is it for now.' Not long after that, we exchanged a few messages on Facebook on the progress of the piece, though last time I checked he had deleted his account, any direct route of contact between us now shut off.

Even then, he'd made me think of Christobal. At first, I thought it sounded ridiculous, but it didn't seem so after a while. They were both young men, lost in their own ways, with responsibilities they couldn't quite get their arms around. They were both just kids, I'd thought to myself, younger than I am now. They both had their struggles, with substances and the general quagmire of rules and binds that make up an adult life. There was no way not to feel sorry for Jason, just as there still isn't any way for me not to feel sorry for Christobal, whatever he might have done, or failed to do.

Several of the main volunteers and workers at Eagles Wings Trust are themselves recovering from addictions of their own, including Tony, a gregarious, strongly built man in his 40s, who was incredibly generous with his time on that first visit. For him, like Christobal, it was drink that took its hold, earlier in his life and it cost him a lot, including friends, family and stability. Now, Eagles Wings is a central part of the born and raised Dundonian's life. He's here every day, rain or shine, along with the others. Tony is also incredibly easy company and we share the same habit of enjoying spinning a good yarn. Frankly, it's always a pleasure to call in on him of an afternoon. It was him and Jason that I was thinking of when I booked to visit Dundee after my strange jaunt in Newcastle, as well as wanting to see what had and hadn't changed in the city since my last trip. On arrival, I checked in to the Queen's Hotel, an imposing old slab of Victorian Gothic in the middle of town, right over the road from the university.

Dundee likes to ham up its status as Scotland's sunniest city, though it wasn't much in evidence as I dropped my bags off in my fourth-floor room and stared out at fat blobs of rain slapping against a churning river Tay. I sent a few texts to my partner and she replied with news about a London heatwave that suddenly felt very far away. The next morning, I made my way up to Douglas Street, for a long overdue catch-up. It felt as strange as it always did, being back in a place with so many memories, with so few of the people I'd shared them with still living in the city. After breakfast I'd walked down to Union Street, where I'd once lived in a grotty student flat for a couple of years, with a bedroom floor that angled sharply south, to make an alarmingly severe slope.

The entire landscape had altered from those days, back in 2013 when I'd upgraded to a more expensive place that had single-glazed windows and shook to its foundations whenever a car passed by at 10 mph outside. In place of a few weathered pubs and the old prefab train station, there was the gleaming V&A and a cluster of new hotels that might as well have been anywhere in Europe. But I wasn't here for nostalgia. This was work and I wanted to see how Tony and the rest of the charity were coping with the new challenges posed by the pandemic. Naturally, the drop-in centre wasn't open but they were still there every day, to hand out packages of food, to whoever needed it. Circumstances might have changed but it hadn't lessened demand, unsurprisingly enough.

On arrival, Tony greeted me like an old friend as we sat down in the back office. He looked well, if tired, in the way that's impossible to mask after months of working flat out, somewhere just beyond normal capacity. 'I'll feel like things are back to normal when I can go to church and sing and when I can go to the football and scream my head off,' he explained as an avid Dundee United fan, when we sat down to talk. He told me that their clientele has become more diverse since my last visit. 'We're seeing a few teachers and nurses coming,' Tony explained. 'It's really like that [now].'

On top of that, there are the sharks circling for the most vulnerable. 'For drug dealers, this place is like honey to a bee. Folk here are in various stages of recovery, taking their scripts and their medicine. You get these chickenhawks coming round and once they have someone back on the heroin it's like turning around a tanker. It'll be another six months to a year before you can get that person back to where they were before. We're not psychologists, but we're just going to hold their hand for a wee while and help sort things out for them.'

Money is tight, just as money is always tight. But just a few weeks before my visit, someone from the local community, they aren't exactly sure who, handed in a £10,000 cheque. 'That's typical of people's generosity and it means rent is sorted out for a couple of months. And that's where we are, always. Making sure that rent and food are paid for.' If you look on the bright side, as Tony often does, then the pandemic can be used as more evidence of a rock-solid community spirit and even the birth of a few opportunities. Something they've been crying out for over the years is more cooperation and communication between services and charities in Dundee. They'd managed to strike up a partnership with the city's parish nursing team since the start of lockdown. 'We split costs. We have a lot of people coming in for help with their utility bills, which is really expensive. It's never less than 20 or 30 quid, or even 50 if you have gas as well as electric in the house. But that's what we're here for. Thankfully, I'm not part of the team that has to worry too much about where the money comes from. It's still a struggle but we aren't going anywhere. Our faith is a big part of that.' There are some cracking stories, Tony stressed to me. 'Just a few weeks ago these two teachers just thought, Let's get off our arses and go for a cycle ride. Let's get folk to sponsor us. 700 quid, they raised,' Tony said, gesturing to another outsized cheque in the main room. 'One of them got his sister to make it.'

But there are some days it can feel like a constant battle, just to keep people from slipping out of sight entirely. The things that people do to get money have long since stopped to shock Tony. For many, things are desperate, all year round. 'Some folk are stretching out 10 or 20 quid's worth of electric for two weeks, just to keep the lights on and maybe a TV. I've been in that situation myself in the past and it's like living in the eighteenth century.' The charity of well-meaning individuals is a good thing, evidence of the depth of community solidarity, but it isn't a replacement for fully funded services. Tony makes no bones about stating what he believes are the roots of Dundee's current troubles. 'We're eroding away that bottom layer of support, that safety net, or whatever you want to call it. That's not news, that's been going on for a couple of decades, from where I've been sitting. But look, we try and stay positive. You've got to when you're coming here every day, because some of those stories you hear are so traumatic. Everybody that walks through that door has a mum and a dad, sisters or brothers that they are separated from through their addiction.' The most important thing is that there is never any judgement. It's an article of their faith, to help and support whoever needs it, whatever is required in that moment. It used to embarrass Tony to put it like that. It sounded too schmaltzy and unlike himself. But that doesn't matter to him now and hasn't for some time.

The doors open at 1 p.m., Monday to Wednesday every week, until 3 p.m. There was already a queue forming just before one, a patient line of people standing a dutiful two metres apart, waiting to take their bag of provisions and for a talk with Tony and some of the other Eagles Wings team members. For the first half an hour, I offered my services handing out the bags of food and making small talk. The line was just as diverse as Tony had said it would be. Old and young, gregarious and quiet, well-turned-out pensioners along with a few slightly glazed younger faces. I kept hoping that Jason would be amongst the crowd, but there was no sign of him while I was there. It was clear that most were regulars, stopping to chat with Barbara, a kindly nurse in her 60s who had been working with the charity since the start of lockdown. We got talking during one of the lulls and she explained that she usually worked with another faith-based organisation in the city and had come to lend a hand when that had closed indefinitely during lockdown. She asked about the book and after I explained what I was doing, there was a definite note of excitement in her voice. 'I met a woman from London up here a while ago. She'd told me she was missing,' Barbara offered hastily. I didn't manage to get any more details out of her as the line started to pick up again and I found myself packing cartons of eggs and packets of tea into carrier bags at a quicker pace than before. Barbara's reaction is something I'd noticed over the many months of reporting. It's remarkable just how many people have a story to tell about the missing. It might be a chance encounter, a lifetime of anguish, or all the other innumerable things that can lie in between. I could tell Barbara's encounter with the missing woman had made quite an impact, but I didn't want to delve in too much. I felt tired, after too much familiarity and too many strange old memories, in a city I didn't feel like I knew all that well anymore.

It felt good to catch up with Tony and help out for an afternoon, so I politely steered the conversation elsewhere and continued to hand out supplies. Soon enough, a man came up with his daughter, who I placed in that awkward moment just before adolescence. They were there for a few bags for their family, his other two kids being at home. Clearly, Barbara and the man had a good rapport and he seemed at ease enough. The girl told me she was going back to school soon and couldn't wait. Imagine that, I replied, a four-month summer holiday. She smiled and dropped her gaze to the ground. The line was beginning to thin out and some of the regulars had clustered along a wall, catching up for a bit of gossip and a smoke, though just a couple of them appeared slightly out of it. After a few more minutes, Tony beckoned me over, producing a cigarette for each of us. After the heavy talk earlier, we kept it mostly to football and halcyon memories of the vastly promising and long since dismantled Dundee United team of the early 2010s, which included a young Andy Robertson, the incredibly durable and talented Liverpool full-back. I remember going to Hampden Park in Glasgow to watch them narrowly lose to Celtic in a Scottish Cup semi-final with my aunty, back in 2013. It was an exhilarating match, right before the precocious youngsters were picked off and transferred to more monied and glamorous clubs. Funny, I said to Tony, the things you remember. The afternoon sky was clouding into rain again, so I started on my goodbyes. Upstairs, I picked up my bag from the main room and saw a framed print on the wall that caught my eye, just by the kitchen. It was Psalm 18:2, the one that sings of a God who is a rock, fortress and stronghold. Who is worthy of praise and can save you from your enemies. On my way to the hotel, I paid attention to the streets to see what memories might surface, of the old and long forgotten days of cheerful irresponsibility.

It wasn't that sort of afternoon. Back in my hotel room, I stood for a bit at the window, looking out at the city centre and beyond, taken right back in my mind's eye to one of the most memorable afternoons I'd ever spent in the city. It was the summer of 2011 and I was with my aunty, standing as two of a teeming crowd at the top of Dundee Law, the steep hill that looms over Dundee like an ancient watch tower. We were there to witness the controlled demolition of a high-rise housing scheme, known locally as the Alexander Street Multis. The flats were rundown and had become notorious, from disinvestment and neglect, though not everyone was happy to see them go. Just how many memories, how many lives, had been bound up in their walls: the imprint of the families that had once called the towers home. There was excitement in the air, something almost feverish and carnivalesque. People huddling together and a crush of camera phones jostling for the best view. At 18, I wasn't really thinking about sadness and regret. It was easy to get swept up with the crowd, just another giddy teenager waiting impatiently on a spectacle. Life is full of novelty, then. But now, I thought of Jason and the family I'd seen earlier at the foodbank. If they'd been there on that overcast Saturday morning nearly a decade ago, cheering along with the rest of us as the detonator sounded and the old buildings crumpled into themselves, their ashes billowing over the city and scattering over the horizon for hours after the explosion. I don't know why it came into my head so many years later and I don't know what it was meant to mean. It's just funny sometimes, the things remembered and all the other things forgotten with them.

CHAPTER 7

They found the body of an unidentified man on 14 November 2015. Two brothers had stumbled on him in the middle of a dense forest at Pentrellyncymer, near Cerrigydrudion in North Wales, as they set up camp ahead of that year's Welsh GB motor rally racing event. Forensics showed he had died from blunt force trauma to the head, several years prior. He was in his 50s, maybe older, perhaps slightly younger. His nose had been fractured at some point, and his bones said he had suffered from arthritis. What the pathologist's careful work couldn't establish was a name – or anything else that could identify the man, to speak to the kind of life that he had led. It didn't take too long for the case to cool. There just weren't enough leads to go off. Of course, the police wanted to give the man a name – but this isn't always possible in the hunt for the missing. And it just gets harder over the weeks and months, as more cases accumulate. More files continue to drop down on the desk, pushing the body in the woods further and further into the past.

To read the press reports is enough to feel a chill running down your back. The violence of the man's death and the absence of supporting context, or even the most basic facts. Who had he been and what actions and accidents had led him to such a sad, squalid end? Who had he left behind, if anyone had even noticed his passing at all? As well as horror, curiosity. How easy and unpleasant to realise the mind running with all the innumerable possibilities. I first came across the story in the early months of 2019 after weeks scouring through the online archives of local papers across the UK, reading about the missing that come to a violent end like the unidentified body in North Wales. The people that have been taken and brought to harm, without anyone ever achieving either justice, peace or even identification. For decades, it was impossible to say exactly how many of these cases lay open at any one time, until the NCA's Missing Persons Unit had published the database of unidentified bodies on their website containing over 1000 cold cases at the start of 2019, with images and a list of unusual features that might help identify the deceased. There are photos taken from the mortuary, distinctive tattoos, or prized possessions – watches, jewellery or whatever was found with the body: man, woman or infant. Some were discovered in the 2010s, others as far back as 1971. There are well-kept faces as well as ghostly sketches and reconstructions. Whenever I scroll through the range of spectres and occasionally grotesque composites, I'm not ashamed to admit the pangs of pity and fright. In my most anxious moments I've tried to set some hope against the thought that this could have been Christobal's fate, until putting the thought as firmly as possible out of mind.

My trips to Manchester and Dundee had shown me the depths of the homelessness crisis and how it was causing people to slip out of sight. But it was just one answer to a question with innumerable answers. Just where was it that the missing were going? The scores of cold cases I'd read about presented another more lurid and macabre explanation. Their impact can feel like it far outstrips their number. What does 1000 look like next to the 180,000 reported missing every year and the hundreds of thousands living with various forms of homelessness? When I'd spoken to Joe Apps about the missing adults who, like Christobal, chose to go missing or absent themselves as 'non-vulnerable' adults, it had boiled down to a question of individual choice. Complicated, often fractured in reasoning, but still a choice, however painful. The taken are not the same. They didn't decide to step outside of their lives in the hope of some strange and fresh beginning. It was done to them, to be taken somewhere else against their will and often done harm to, like the body in the woodlands of North Wales.

Our culture is full of their reverberations. From the endless words devoted to speculation about the whereabouts of long-term mispers like Suzy Lamplugh, the west London estate agent who went to meet a client on 28 July 1986 and was never seen again. Every so often, an article will appear online with her story as part of a compilation of the UK's most notorious unsolved crimes, usually bereft of any new information or breakthroughs. All these years later it still carries a half-repelled fascination: guaranteed eyes and traffic for whichever tabloid has decided to run it this time. Our collective fascination with true crime has propelled a global boom in the genre over the past decade, with endless glossy Netflix documentaries, podcasts and blockbuster non-fiction books, from *Making a Murderer* and *Serial* to *I'll Be Gone in the Dark: One Woman's Obsessive Search for the Golden State Killer* by the late Michelle McNamara. There's nothing new about this preoccupation with murder and human wickedness. There's a well-documented lineage running from the cheap sensationalism of the eighteenth- and nineteenth-century penny dreadfuls to the big-budget offerings of today, cloaked by their knowing seriousness and the respectability of the consultant criminologists employed to give the enterprise an added sheen of professionalism. Their popularity can be partly explained by the need to understand what, according to American forensic psychologist Dr Paul G. Mattiuzzi, is 'a most fundamental taboo and also, perhaps, a most fundamental human impulse'.

It's a grim compulsion I've sometimes found myself guilty of, even if I've occasionally tried to dress it up in the professional justification of it being linked to my work, both in this book and elsewhere. In the early autumn of 2020 I'd sat down to watch David Tennant in *Des*, the ITV miniseries detailing the capture of, and subsequent media frenzy around, the serial killer Dennis Nilsen, who murdered at least 12 young men between 1978 and 1983 from his two north London addresses. His victims were mostly lonely, troubled boys lured back with the promise of a drink and some company for the night. Some of them had spent time missing before their fateful encounters with Nilsen. Vulnerable people, living life on the margins of the city. Of his confirmed victims, several have never been identified. There just wasn't enough to go off, despite the intensity of the search. They are still missing, their identities lost, likely for ever.

I didn't know all that much about Nilsen and his victims until the programme aired and I quickly found myself obsessively reading all the available facts over the subsequent weeks. I'm still not sure why, but a few weeks later I'd found myself catching a succession of unfamiliar trains and buses up to Muswell Hill, the neighbourhood where Nilsen had lived at Flat 23D, Cranley Gardens. It was there that the discovery of discoloured and rotted human flesh had been made in a clogged drain, which had led to his arrest. The area itself is a study in residential north London boredom, full of grand Edwardian houses and fussy little cafes. I'd ventured up there on a dismal Wednesday afternoon in the hope of something I didn't really want to articulate until later. Standing on the street, looking up at the top floor of the unprepossessing mock Tudor conversion wasn't going to offer any worthwhile insights. I had nothing new or revelatory to say about the case. The thought of the still missing men who had died didn't require my trekking miles across the city to peer up at the little attic flat of horrors. Before turning back, I felt a pang of shame at the curiosity that had led me there. Sometimes in my journey through the world of the missing, it felt right to follow an impulse, but the opposite could also be true.

Of all the ways that people can be taken and suppressed from sight, there is one I couldn't stop obsessing over. My fixation began in the autumn of 2019 when I'd read about the story of a man called Michael, though that was a pseudonym. He had been living on the streets when a couple approached him to sell drugs. It meant the chance to make something like a living, in a life that had filled up with desperation. The BBC reported how the then 34-year-old was treated well at the beginning by the couple. It didn't stay that way for long. It didn't seem to matter how much money he made, Michael told how the couple would say he owed them more and more. He was always behind, chasing his own debts, falling further and further into them. Things spiralled. Soon, they had taken the card that his benefits were paid into. He was trapped. And one day, the couple threw him into the back of a van and took him to a strange address where he was forced to carry on working, unpaid. Michael had been enslaved. Though not a new concern, the number of recorded modern slavery offences has steeply risen in the UK over the past decade. In the year ending March 2019 there were 5,144 such offences recorded by the police in England and Wales, an increase of 51 per cent from the previous year, while the independent Modern Slavery Helpline received a 68 per cent increase in calls and submissions in the year ending December 2018, compared with the year before. These figures are thought by almost everyone in the field to be a significant underestimate, just like the 180,000 reported missing. In 2016, Global Slavery Index estimated that there were 136,000 people in the UK living in modern slavery on any given day.[15] Almost a quarter are, like Michael, British nationals. The rest are an international mixture of people lured with the promise of non-existent legal employment. Others are simply taken from their home country and deposited here, to sell drugs, tend to cannabis grow houses or forced into agricultural labour by their slave masters, who hail – just like their victims – from Vietnam, Eastern Europe and almost any continent you care to name.

It is an evil present in every corner of the UK. Like the rest of the missing, they are invisible. Here but not here, somewhere just out of sight. But they didn't slip quietly from view of their own volition. They are hidden to us, locked out of their own lives. The stories we encounter are those of the people who have been found, just as Michael had been. Perhaps they managed to escape or were rescued. Their testimony is all that we have to go on. It's likely that we walked past people trapped in slavery every week. It might be the men working in the cash-in-hand carwash in town, or held in a house the next street over. It could be the cleaner that moves through your empty office at night, or

the woman who silently gives you your inexpensive manicure at the local beautician's on the high street. It is hard to
know exactly. Our lives are full of unthinking convenience.
How closely do we ever tend to look at the foundations
that underpin it? It is a convenience that has its consequences. According to the charity Anti-Slavery, forced
labour is the most common form of slavery in the UK,
driven for our collective desire for cheap services and
consumer goods. 'Hidden in plain sight' is a term that has
caught on over the past few years to describe the plight of
the enslaved and trafficked, as well as their captors. It made
me consider Christobal's early life here afresh. How he had
fallen into dubious cash-in-hand employment, at the mercy
of unscrupulous employers in the legal and moral never-
never land of the grey economy. He had been young and
naive, with a variable hold on the language. The precise sort
of figure ripe for exploitation. But there was a crucial difference. Though vulnerable, he wasn't alone. He had Mum
and the rest of our family to keep him in sight and stop
things progressing too far.

In the early autumn of 2020, I spoke with Caroline
Haughey QC, one of the UK's leading experts on modern
slavery. Having prosecuted the first such cases in the country, she was invited to assist the All Party Parliamentary
Group on Human Trafficking and Modern Slavery in
proposing what became the 2015 Modern Slavery Act, the
first legislation of its kind in the UK. It took a while for us
to set a time to talk, as there were trials to be prepared

fought and prepared for. I'd first become aware of Caroline's work in the summer of 2019, when I'd read about her role as successful lead prosecutor in Operation Fort, a sprawling case brought against what had been dubbed the biggest modern slavery network that had ever been uncovered in the UK. Five men and three women were sentenced to decades in prison for their role in a Polish organised crime network that police believed might have had more than 400 victims in the West Midlands. Putting together the case was a long, arduous process. It had taken four years to bring it to trial. The group had targeted the most desperate from their homeland, including rough sleepers, as well as ex-prisoners and people suffering from substance abuse issues. It would start with a promise of decent work and accommodation: the chance of a new life and fresh start, far away from their problems back home. After arriving in the UK by coach, they'd be spirited away to discover the reality. Their housing was squalid, almost beyond imagination, spread out across the towns of West Bromwich, Walsall and Smethwick, forced up to four in a room to sleep on rancid mattresses. One victim later reported that he had to wash in a nearby canal, as there was no running water. The work itself proved backbreaking and incessant. Long, grinding days on local farms and turkey-gutting factories, with the wages immediately siphoned off by the gang on pay day. Their passports had been seized, making escape impossible. And without any English, their captors' lies were gospel. What, they'd threaten, are you going to tell the police as a paperless illegal immigrant? It is our word against yours. We are powerful, you are nothing. You will be deported or thrown in prison if you talk. And if you run, we will kill you or make sure your family comes to harm back home. In public, their captors cultivated a respectable face, working to convince banks and employment agencies of their good character. They were organised and efficient. One member would travel to Poland to groom potential victims, while others would be in charge of finances and setting up fraudulent benefit claims using their captives' identities. The wife of one of the gang's leaders would even fulfil a carefully acted role as welcoming matriarch, soothing new arrivals, making them food and cups of tea, listening sweetly to their stories of home and dreams for the future, knowing precisely what cruelty and horror lay in store. At trial, it came to light that a total of 92 victims had been identified. The true number, police suggested, ran to hundreds more, but they couldn't be traced, had left the country or were too frightened of the consequences to give evidence. They were still the missing, with their very existence buried from view.

'I'm an odd person,' Caroline told me over the phone from the sideline of her daughter's hockey match, 'in that I'm what I'd call a "pracademic". I'm a practitioner first and foremost, but because of my role in the inception of the act I'm now also writing and lecturing with academics. I do quite a lot of thought stuff, for want of a better description.' In her teaching, which involves nationwide training for prosecutors as well as governments abroad, she makes sure

to place emphasis on one crucial point. 'When I'm prosecut-
ing a slavery case, it's the evidence of absence, as much as
the evidence of presence [that is important], which goes to
what you're [writing] about.' Caroline pointed to another
case she'd been part of that had involved trafficked
Vietnamese girls working in nail bars across the country.
'The really compelling evidence was the fact that there was
no record of their existence. Everyone has a digital footprint. When you're born, there's registration of your birth,
an NHS record or at least something. The amount of people
not born under medical guidance [in the UK] is less than
0.1 per cent,' Caroline explained. 'But if you come into this
jurisdiction without papers, you haven't been educated
here, or registered with the local authority, then you don't
exist. Hiding someone in plain sight is then really flipping
easy. There are lots of missing people. In fact, in every slavery case I've done, the absence of evidence point is a
significant issue.' Bank details and transactions, social
media accounts: when these and other signs of activity
don't exist, then the next question is what, or who, has
crafted that absence? There is a hole where the ephemera of
a life should be. The victim who has been rescued is physically present, so what has happened to the thousand little
things that were supposed to keep track of their movements
and speak to the fact of their existence that they have led
here in the UK?

'When someone falls victim to modern slavery or
exploitation, it is because there is a vulnerability in their

life. That might be something that's innate. It might be mental health related, or something that's foisted on them by circumstances,' Caroline continued. I told her it reminded me precisely of the missing more generally. Something had gone wrong in the life of the missing person. And it isn't always something they could control, or that even stays still long enough to diagnose. '[Yes] it might be changing [all the time]. Whatever it is, it's something that can be exploited by the perpetrator. One vulnerability perpetuates another.' With the Polish nationals in the West Midlands, their recruitment centred around money and the promise of a better life. They were offered reasonable jobs, 'but it was never a golden handshake. [They were told] if you come to the UK, you will be sorting rubbish, etc., but we'll give you accommodation and pay you £300 a week. Can you imagine what that is to someone who's earning £100 a week? Or they might not be earning any money because they have alcohol and drug issues, or mental health problems. Maybe they've been in prison due to all of the above. Or maybe it's just someone who wants to financially improve themselves.' There is also the question of responsibility. The gang and their victims were not something separate from society, a frightening aberration that existed somewhere outside of its walls. Clandestine and repressed from view, yes, but not the other. Their forced labour was indirectly used by some of the UK's biggest supermarket chains. 'Now, they'd delegated the employment of those people to an agency and had done the basic due diligence.

But after that, they'd been absolved of responsibility,' Catherine said. '[And] ask your teenage girl who is going to get a manicure before a night out and pays six quid. People aren't prepared to acknowledge that if you want it cheaper and faster then there is a cost. The human cost is people who are vulnerable to exploitation because they're the ones who work for less for longer.'

In the days that passed after my interview with Caroline Haughey, I was mostly engaged with the usual business of research. Trying to put together the picture of modern slavery in the UK and where it sat in the uneven mosaic of the missing persons crisis. The stories kept accumulating. There were the Vietnamese teenage boys trafficked to the UK and enslaved on makeshift cannabis farms and how, despite the much trumpeted introduction of the Modern Slavery Act in 2015, funding for survivors had been cut by 42 per cent,[16] with thousands of child-trafficking victims denied the right to remain in the country. My notebook had started to fill with similar horrors and I thought about how lucky I was to be able to push them aside and head out for a walk on a crisp autumnal late afternoon.

When things are stressful, I like to put an old photograph of me and Christobal next to my laptop. I don't know why, but it can help my mind stay in focus, like I'm working towards him and his Spanish homeland, his visage keeping me company on my journey through the missing. It's one of my favourites, the two of us clad all in red, looking like a team of Santa's most recalcitrant helpers. Our faces have

been caught out by the flash, giving the illusion of a candid moment interrupted by the photographer. There's no way the image captures me anywhere older than 18 months and he must be about 23, if my calculations are correct, his thick black hair whipped up as if he'd been caught out in the wind. That afternoon, I placed it carefully in my shirt pocket as I headed out, as if it were a lucky charm. After a few miles I found myself turning through Ladywell Fields and off to Hither Green, the area where we had that first flat, me, him and Mum together. It's not an area with very much to see, a twist of respectable arterial roads and a few single-decker bus routes. After an hour, I realised that I didn't know the address of our old flat anymore and didn't have reason to head there even if I had. Instead, I picked up my pace and found myself a quiet little cafe on Staplehurst Road. Though not quite the only customer, it was slow inside with the sense of things winding up for the day. The sort of time when all manner of absurd thoughts are liable to flash around your brain. When Christobal had lived here, it must have been the era of his trouble with work as a young man, ripped off and exploited by the sharks who would have seen him coming a mile off. I felt a swell of paternal anger, as if he was my son and not the other way around. I wished I could have protected him against the vultures, as if I was the one to have failed in my duty of care. The coffee was too strong and my head had begun to pulse. On the journey home, I stopped for a cigarette in Crofton Park and watched as a middle-aged woman fussed around with the recycling on her doorstep. She'd left the front door ajar as I tried to resist the stupid urge to stare into the hallway. The heavy brown door soon swung shut and the woman disappeared behind it. Just another of the million glimpses into lives we know nothing about.

CHAPTER 8

The missing appear to add another coating of intrigue and suspense to the true-life stories we consume. A week or so after my talk with Caroline Haughey, I finally sat down to watch *The Disappearance of Madeleine McCann*, the eight-part Netflix documentary series from 2019, which had become one of the streaming platform's most watched releases of the year, despite the case being well over a decade old. It's a slick production that sets down the familiar outline of the then three-year-old's disappearance from a holiday resort in the Algarve, during a trip with her parents Kate and Gerry McCann. The critical response was mixed. The *Guardian* called it 'a blatant cash-in on the vogue for the true-crime series that have become a staple of Netflix's output ... but without any of the justifications previous works in the genre have provided'. The reviewer couldn't see the point of a series that '[wasn't] the disinterment of a forgotten case [or] the re-examination of a suspected miscarriage of justice. It offered no new facts, no new insight. It didn't even have a point of view.' It's a scathing piece of writing, an evisceration wrapped up in the guise of critique, the moral distaste dripping off the page. My own feelings weren't as strong. True, there was little in the way of revelation or new information in the series. It is, after all, arguably the best-known unsolved missing persons case in the world. Every year seems to throw up a new spate of headlines and a drip feed of new sightings and potential leads, the public appetite for which still appears to be inexhaustible. (Since the documentary was made police have identified a German man already in prison as the new prime suspect.) The documentary's success struck me as just further confirmation of the cultural power carried by a certain type of missing, particularly when it came to certain kinds of missing children. Though that might well be a significant underselling of their impact. There's something more to it than an effect on TV ratings or tabloid sales. The depth of emotions conjured by a particularly tragic case can even become a political force. Back in the early 2010s at the height of the News International phone-hacking scandal, it wasn't the steady flow of celebrities and public figures coming forward with their tales of press skulduggery and intrusion into their private lives that really ignited the full scale of public revulsion that precipitated the Leveson Inquiry, which delved into darkest practices of a corner of the British press. Instead, it was the revelation in July 2011 that an 'investigator' working for the *News of the World* had hacked into the mobile phone of Milly Dowler, the Surrey schoolgirl who had been found murdered in

September 2002, five months after she had been abducted. The shameful nature of the intrusion precipitated a wave of shock and disgust that culminated in Rupert Murdoch himself meeting with the Dowlers to offer a personal apology.

At the start of my reporting and research into the missing, most of my attention had been centred on missing adults, perhaps a consequence of my own past and thoughts of Christobal, though partly because of how alarming I'd found the paucity of meaningful public attention surrounding the issue. Missing children felt like something else again. Another shadowy world of hunches and incomplete information. Of the 180,000 people that are reported missing every year, around 76,000 are children. The number of what are called 'missing incidents' is significantly higher at around 353,000 according to Missing People. This discrepancy is due to the individuals who go missing repeatedly, with children accounting for around 220,000[17] of these recorded incidents. It's thought that one in 200 children go missing in the UK every year. For those who fall into the category of 'looked after children' (defined as any child in local authority care for more than 24 hours) that figure jumps to one in ten. The term is usually applied interchangeably with 'children in care', which at least according to the National Society for the Prevention of Cruelty to Children is one that the young people themselves often prefer. The number of children in the English care system has ballooned by 28 per cent over the last decade. In 2010 the figure stood at 60,900. In January 2020, it had risen to 78,150.[18] The Local Government Association has since warned of the pressures created by the increase in demand that combined with funding shortages have meant more and more vulnerable young people slipping through the cracks of a system increasingly unfit for purpose. Just as the overall number of children in care has grown, so have the numbers that disappear from the system and become missing children, for however long it is until they are located again. Between 2015 and 2018, the numbers of young people going missing from care doubled. One of the key drivers has been the entrenchment of 'out-of-area placements', when looked after children are sent to accommodation far from their home local authority, with thousands placed more than 100 miles away. I wasn't long into my reading about missing children when the term first presented itself. Between 2012 and 2018 the number of these placements grew by 61 per cent from 2,250 children in 2012 to 3,990 in 2018,[19] despite the government's own advice that they should only be utilised as a last resort, unless in the child's best interests.

The problems with their growing prevalence are clear, according to a House of Commons research briefing published in February 2020. Being so far away from home can be traumatic for young people who already experienced difficult upbringings. Just because they are being looked after, it doesn't mean that they should be removed from everything they've ever known and whatever support networks they have. It can incubate the kind of isolation that increases the risks of going missing. And for those that do the risks are profound, including criminal and sexual exploitation. One teenage girl, who was placed 150 miles from home, features as part of a report by the Children's Commissioner for England and described her experience of feeling 'like a parcel getting moved around all the time, getting opened up and sent back and moved on to somewhere else'. More than half of those living out of area have special educational needs, while a quarter were reported as having social, emotional and mental health issues. The added instability in their lives sees the stress build. And what fear does running away hold when you have already been displaced from anything you thought you knew?

Ann Coffey is the former long-serving Labour MP for Stockport and served as the chair of the All-Party Parliamentary Group for Runaway and Missing Children and Adults between 2010 and 2019. I'd been familiar with the group's work from the late summer of 2019 when I'd read about their inquiry into the record numbers of children going missing from care in England. The APPG had argued that out-of-area placements were having the effect of making looked after young people more, not less, vulnerable to potential criminal exploitation. The inquiry found that 70 per cent of 41[20] police forces surveyed said placing children out of area enhanced their risk of exploitation and resulted in them being coerced into going missing. Something had clearly gone drastically wrong in a system that rarely tends to enter into the public eye unless in the form of a particularly egregious crisis. Adolescents in care don't often tend to muster the same pitch of emotional response as telegenic disappeared or abducted small children. They are difficult and awkward, often exhibiting challenging behaviours, and are unlikely to be typecast as angels or cyphers for a lost innocence like Madeleine McCann.

Occasionally, a scandal breaks through into the national consciousness. In January 2011, *The Times* began to publish a series of stories into decades of child sexual exploitation in Rotherham, South Yorkshire. Between the end of the 1980s and the 2010s, they detailed how local authorities had failed to act on reports of abuse by grooming gangs who preyed on vulnerable young girls from chaotic backgrounds, many of whom were living in local children's homes. It was soon followed by the similar scandal in Rochdale, where nine men were convicted of child sex trafficking in May 2012. Both stories document a catalogue of horrors and a string of failures by local police and child protection agencies. It later transpired that many of the victims had reported their abuse, only to be discounted as unreliable witnesses. Both stories sparked a national debate about the racial motivation of the crimes, as the majority of perpetrators were men of South Asian descent and most of the victims white. What resulted sometimes had the flavour of a moral panic, obscuring some of underlying issues around the crimes and the systems that had failed the victims so appallingly.

When I spoke to Ann Coffey she started our conversation by explaining how, supported by both Missing People and The Children's Society, the APPG's twin responsibilities meant having to publish separate reports, 'as the statutory responsibilities are just [so] different [for children and adults]. We became very interested in the vulnerability of children to grooming and, of course, children in care are particularly vulnerable,' she said over video link from her home in south London. In 2012, another report had been published by the group with a raft of recommendations, with the Conservative government of the time implementing a set of procedures that did little to alleviate the problems that had been diagnosed, including an unmet pledge to reduce the amount of out-of-area placements. '[Not] many of them really worked because the fundamental problem was the structure of children's homes. Ironically, it might have got worse because local authorities started to justify these out-of-area placements as being in the interest of the children.'

The argument in favour of out-of-area placements runs that it's better for a child exhibiting worrying signs of being involved in criminality or in danger of being groomed by older gangs in their local area to be taken away, before matters can get any worse. It's true that there are times when they present the only plausible option. When a child is at risk in their local area, with all other routes exhausted, then removal can be the best safeguarding policy. There's also the matter of cost. Perhaps not coincidentally, out-of-area placements are also by far the less expensive option than providing provision where it's needed the most. Between 2015 and 2020 the number of children's homes in London and the South East shrunk by 3 per cent despite a 12 per cent overall increase[21] in the number of children in care. While the South has struggled for space, other areas have a relative glut of homes. The North West, as well as the East and West Midlands saw a significant increase, with 60 new children's homes built in the North West in the same five-year period. Many of them are unregulated, which means children often aged 16 or 17, often living almost entirely unsupported. Others are unregistered, beyond the vision of Ofsted or other regulators. Though the first kind of home is legal, the latter isn't – an important semantic distinction. 'Providers have set up homes in the same area as they can manage things like staff absences and training much more easily. But [these are also] places where housing provision is cheaper,' Ann said, pointing to a provider in Rochdale as an example. 'It doesn't cost a lot to buy a terraced house there. Whatever the reason, the end result is that around 70 per cent of children's homes are in the private sector and the accommodation is not where children coming into the care system need it to be. Without tackling this you aren't going to tackle the issue of moving children away from their home community. [For many] there just isn't the provision locally.'

For hard-up local authorities battered by budgetary cuts and over a decade of enforced austerity measures, it might appear a simple call to let private providers take on the responsibility. '[They have] opted out of providing direct services, which is very expensive for them. It just leaves them vulnerable to escalating prices, a bit like the adult social care system,' Ann explained to me. 'Children who come into care are likely to be vulnerable,' she repeated, 'particularly when they come into children's homes. It makes it very difficult for them to get any benefit from education. Usually mental health facilities aren't available because of funding problems. [Out-of-area placements] make it very difficult for family members, or extended members of that family, to keep in contact. Effectively what you're doing is disrupting that child's contacts. It may be that their parents are tossers, right? But it might be that somewhere in that family there is a connection. Whatever it is, children love their families. We then get surprised that the outcome isn't good. We're taking children into care because we're concerned about their welfare, but we're putting them into a system that puts them at risk. Of course the children go missing.'

I asked Ann what could be done, to stem the numbers of at-risk children perilously close to falling out of vision. It wasn't, she said, that the issue continues to languish undiagnosed. 'The problem isn't that the Department for Education doesn't understand the problem or doesn't know that it needs fixing. They just won't fix it. They would have to take over the responsibility for ensuring that there were places nationwide. Local authorities can't do that. They have a statutory responsibility to ensure there are sufficient places in their local area, but they can't always do that with children coming into the area.' The answer isn't that difficult, Anna told me. In Greater Manchester, both Wigan and Rochdale's local authorities managed to secure funding. 'They worked with young girls who were being sexually exploited or were at risk of sexual exploitation and were at the edge of coming into the care system. They recruited social workers to work with these young people on the priorities that these young people had. When it was evaluated it was found to be quite successful and saved them an arm and a leg.' If central government was clear with local authorities and their responsibility to provide local places, she continued, the difference would be pronounced. 'Local authorities have access to social housing, etc. If they had funding to make a change to the model, then change could happen. But [the government] aren't willing to do it. The answer to that is that at the end of the day, people don't care about children [in care].'

My talk with Ann had triggered something from my own past, an event and a childhood friendship I've never known quite what to do with in adulthood. I think about G a lot these days, though there was a time when I didn't at all. The deeper I went into the missing children in care, the more he visited me in my daydreams. We'd been close from the beginning at primary school. We had things in common, besides an aptitude for Nintendo all-nighters. Christobal the drunk. His dad, the drug addict. My memories of G are so deep and so blurred that it always comes as a shock to think how he would have been present in that moment of time when I lived with both Mum and Christobal in the basement flat in Forest Hill. So far back that it stretches almost beyond words. I think we must have been 14 or so, one oppressively hot summer's night in 2006 when I was back, staying at my gran's. He lived nearby in a crumbling Victorian house – a place where it felt like there was always some kind of chaos ready to kick off. Though never in care, home wasn't a place he always wanted to be. G had a cousin in north London, where he'd go to escape from his dad's occasional visitations. There had also been a phone call that night, as we stood around, doing close to fuck-all, accompanied by his mother's tears. His dad was round the house again, she said, leathering the door, yelling for money, screaming against his real and imagined enemies. No, she wasn't frightened, but it might be best for you not to come home until he exhausted himself and drifted off again. How do teenage boys react when faced with phone calls like that? Embarrassment, mainly. Anger. You feel all sorts of things, then. He decided to walk all the way to his cousin's, right there and then. I didn't argue or point out that it was miles away, without an Oyster Card or directions. When G got these things in his head, you knew better than to remonstrate. A thousand times you'd seen it. There would be a trigger, a switch, or whatever. Then the decisive action, swift and streamlined as you like. He was good like that, always clear in judgement. Always precise, no matter the consequences.

The image in the memory, in my imagination, is of standing at the peak of Forest Hill Road looking down into the horizon, at the mess of traffic and tall buildings, trying to track G's progress long after he'd left my vision. His angular, adolescent figure lost in the summer haze as he propelled north through the city in a straight line of hazard and noise. I've always wondered what his route was, a friend I have never been able to imagine further than the confines of that street, let alone Forest Hill. Did he check down the Old Kent Road and over Waterloo Bridge and up through Holborn? Or was it a custom route, full of illogical detours and the chance idiosyncrasies? Through my adult eyes I can see what I'd never have understood then, the figure of a vulnerable boy fleeing the instability of home to a temporary sanctuary. Vulnerability isn't in the lexicon of most teenage boys, however obvious it might seem now. It's the last descriptor I'd have wished on myself or my friends from childhood. For those brief hours, on his journey between home and somewhere else, I suppose he was just another potential missing child, right up until he wasn't.

So many summers have passed that I can't be sure how much I've got wrong or right in my telling now, or even if it's quite my story to relate. We never spoke of it again. There was no desire to pull it apart and impute some deeper meaning to his apparently snap decision. Not everything can be pulled apart and scavenged for significance. Eventually G had arrived safely at his cousin's flat and that was the end of it, for that day at least. Like so many of the other children who go missing, he had only been temporarily out of vision. Though he hadn't come to harm, another few inches in either direction on that strange summer night and things could have been catastrophically different. The fine margins and chance that can turn a temporarily missing person into a long-term case. Sometimes I wonder what I'd say to G if I bumped into him while running some errands back in Forest Hill. It's not an implausible thought. A few years ago I heard from a close mutual friend that G was doing well, though it was light on illuminating detail apart from the fact he still lived in the area. It was just enough to feel relief. Many days have come when I've thought about reaching out, to reconnect with him and talk over all the things that happened and discover something about the life he's led since. But I've never quite managed to get that far, despite knowing it would only take a few phone calls or perfunctory searches on social media. That knowledge again, which only comes with experience and the accumulated petty disappointments of any life. What if the reunion fell flat? What if his capacity for nostalgia was less than my own, our conversation dissolving into awkwardness after the initial bursts of remember whens? There is no guarantee that his vision of the past would chime with or even complement my own, or that the idea that he'd been a borderline missing person wouldn't still feel like a blatant absurdity. It seems so very far away now and really, it's perhaps only right that it should. Sometimes I like to fantasise about what would have happened if I'd followed him that night, a concrete gesture of companionship to let him know that he wasn't alone in the way his actions seemed to suggest. But I know it's an opportunity that won't present itself again and it can feel sad, for just as long as the memory holds at all.

There was something else that Ann had mentioned and that continually cropped up in reports about the dangers that often befell missing children such as those who disappear from the semi-regulated world of out-of-area placements. I'd heard about the dangers of children going missing due to criminal exploitation and wanted to know more about exactly where it was they were going.

Almost every report mentioned county lines, a term that has gradually eased its way into the mainstream press over the past few years. The NCA's definition of the term is clear. County lines is where illegal drugs are transported from one area to another, from major cities out into provincial towns and the countryside, often across police and local authority boundaries (although not exclusively), usually by children or vulnerable people who are coerced into it by the gangs. The county line refers to the mobile line that keeps the operation running like clockwork, day and night. Crack and heroin are the staple products on sale. Recruitment can start on the local estate, at school or over social media. There's the promise of easy money, for what might seem like a simple trade: a few days away in an unfamiliar town. Most recruits are in their teens, though some reports point to children as young as eight having been involved in some capacity. For the drug gangs, the benefits are clear. Children are often targeted because they are less likely to be known to law enforcement and are more likely to receive lenient sentences if and when they are caught. In practice, it has meant an ever growing stream of young people from the UK's biggest cities, like London and Liverpool, being sent out to almost every corner of the country, from Southend to Aberdeen, to serve as cogs in the local drug markets. The reality on arrival is a world of violence and squalor. If things go wrong, the consequences are immediate and severe. If drugs or money go missing, it is the young runners who bear the brunt. Beatings and stabbings are common. One former dealer referenced in a 2018 Community Care article outlined how he was stabbed in the legs and arms 'as a warning' when he told his higher-ups that he wanted out. It is fairly common for the gang's leaders to set up the new recruits, staging robberies to make sure they fall ever further into debts that can't be paid back as a means of further binding them into their new predicament. Work by the NCA identified hundreds of county lines[22] operations around the country, though the picture rarely stays static long enough to gauge precisely.

Escaping the grinding routine of 'going country' isn't a straightforward process. Once you're in, it's difficult to get out. One trip turns to two, turns to months of the same cycle. For some of the young people involved, their absence will hardly be remarked upon, their home lives too chaotic for it to even register. They are lost, have slipped between the cracks of the strained services that should be keeping them in sight. For others who do have distraught families left behind, the prospects can be just as challenging. In October 2020, I picked up on a story involving a 15-year-old boy who had been stabbed after he moved 100 miles away from home to escape the clutches of the gang he had been recruited by. He'd been sent from London to another corner of the South East, where he'd been attacked after his mother accused social services of leaving her son 'high and dry'. There had been official confusion and a catalogue of misunderstandings, as his new local authority refused him a social worker, as he already had one in his home borough. Wires had crossed and responsibility passed on and deferred, with terrible consequences. Moving away hadn't been enough, with the gang's tentacles extending to his new home. The boy had been lost in his shuffle across the country, just like the thousands placed in out-of-area placements. '[His] social worker in the old area wouldn't commit to the commute to come [and make] the statutory visits he was supposed to [make], so we were just left,' said the boy's mother, quoted in the BBC report. In November 2018, an article in social care trade magazine *Community Care* outlined how the experience of former dealers whose experience in children's homes and pupil referral units made them easy pickings for gangs and how even well-meaning social workers could be 'out of their depth' in trying to stage an intervention.

In July 2020, I'd met with journalist Max Daly at a quiet pub off a nondescript backstreet near London Bridge as the summer heat was at its late afternoon peak. Despite it being our first face-to-face meeting, we'd already known each other for years through an email-heavy professional context. Max is Global Drugs Editor at VICE as well as one of the UK's most astute reporters on his beat. In 2019, he won the prestigious Orwell Prize for his work on a series of features on county lines, including a piece on the link between missing children and this particular corner of the UK drug trade. Max is also the editor responsible for sending me to Dundee to write my feature on drug-tested deaths in the city back in 2018, where I'd first met Tony and the crew of volunteers at Eagles Wings Trust. After a bit of small talk, we got straight down to it. '[Going country] is so risky and these young people are stuck between a rock and a hard place. They have their bosses who are sometimes arseholes, their rivals, the police. It's not a joyous place to be. I wanted to put it in context a bit. Throughout history, children have been exploited to do all sorts of criminal stuff. Every single crime you can imagine. County lines just happens to be the big one in the modern era.' Though the model is relatively new, the impulse behind it isn't. 'From the year dot people have been selling drugs from the bigger cities in small places. That's just distribution,' Max said as our drinks arrived on what was turning into a close, muggy evening. Through his reporting, he told me that he managed to accurately trace the origins of teenagers being used by gangs to go and sell drugs in satellite towns and seaside resorts. '[It started in] Brighton in 1999. I went through various sources, through people who were selling at that time and police in the area at that time. That was pretty much [the beginning]. It was a few young black kids from Brixton who had gone to Brighton. It was the first proper set-up.' One heroin user from the time told Max of his shock back then. 'He said he was used to middle-aged Scousers or user dealers. Suddenly there were these little kids on BMXs. They were very swift and professional. Cheaper drugs and clearly controlled by a manager. They thought [the users] were scumbags and would almost chuck the drugs on the ground.' Brighton wasn't the only seaside destination for the early wave of county lines gangs. By the late 2000s, gangs from all over London were staples on the streets of other southern coastal towns, ranging from Bournemouth to Ipswich. The youths ranging from their early teens to early 20s weren't just bringing hard drugs with them. As Max has written, the expansion of the urban drug trade 'into rural and coastal areas was signposted by a rise in supplanted urban violence. It was no coincidence, for example, that the rise of London gangs selling in Southend led to a steep rise in stabbings and shootings.' Just as in the city, there were battles over turf and control of the local drug markets, as well as personal beefs that had just spilled over into a new setting.

As I reread through Max's pieces, it was impossible to ignore the link between county lines and the ever escalating numbers of missing children. Social media played a key role, though not quite in the same way I'd seen when talking to Joe and Kirsty at Missing People. Police would post their appeals in the typical way. In October 2017, the Met had issued a plea for information for the whereabouts of a 15-year-old north London teenager. The teenager's mugshot was quickly amplified on Snapchat by a friend, with 'Man's gone cunch!' plastered in capitals above it. Just a couple of months later, media reports emerged of nine alarming teenage disappearances in Enfield, the sprawling north London borough. It was impossible to say if the cases were linked, but there were a few common denominators. They were all boys, predominantly black and aged between 13 and 17. The online response to the vanishings soon took on a life of its own. Had they been abducted by some deranged killer? The truth was that at least one of the missing boys was out in the countryside, selling drugs day and night from a flat in Boston, Lincolnshire. He was eventually rescued after his family broadcast their own social media appeal and he was found by two locals in the town, mercifully unharmed but clearly frightened.

What had led him to that point? There is something that often gets lost in the more sensationalist coverage devoted to county lines. Among all the breathless column inches that present a narrative of quaint Little England invaded by the evils of the inner city, very little attention seems to focus on the facts and circumstances of the children themselves. And the fact is that these are the vulnerable children that Ann Coffey and others had described. Some will have been plucked from the crumbling care system. Others will have been recruited from nearby their homes. To the elders they work for, their lives and wellbeing can mean almost nothing. If they are arrested or fall prey to violence, they are easy to replace. I tried to think about what it must feel like, living with that anxiety and every day, so far from home. It must be a profound psychological dislocation, Max had said, 'For a kid of 13 or 14, who has spent their entire life in inner-city London, that is suddenly taken into some weird country or seaside town full of white people, it must seem like you've been beamed into a different planet. How do those kids deal with that situation, when they've been dumped into that place?' One academic study into county lines in Southend and Plymouth showed that most of the violence that went with the imported drug trade was done to the young runners themselves, the young teens right at the very bottom of the food chain. 'It wasn't by the runners to the drug users, though [that happens] too. It was more like the local users and dealers kicking the shit out of these little kids. It's like, look, they have money and they're school kids [it doesn't take] much.' For the families left behind, it is just as much of a nightmare. 'It's a very violent world they've been taken into. It's not just police or their rivals, it's the people that they're selling to. And unless something changes then it just keeps on happening.'

There's an easy trap to fall into as someone working from the outside, adult world, looking into the lives of the inner-city children who end up missing, far from home and living in often unspeakably violent, harrowing conditions in dingy crack houses across the country. Though coercion and criminal exploitation undoubtedly play a more than significant part, not every teenager going country has been forced into it. It might be that prospects at home are bleak or non-existent. It comes back to the spiralling child poverty rates that show just how much harder things have become for so many in the past decade and more, a perfect storm occasioned by austerity and swingeing cuts to youth services around the country. What did it say about the health of our society, when so many young people see the dangers of going country as the best route to earn a living? For others, there is also the temptation of the status it can confer. It's not a straightforward picture, as Max and others outlined to me. In early 2020, a Home Office report in the UK drug trade noted the complexity of county lines, drawing on the testimony of frontline youth workers. There are, the report stated, 'elements of conscious choice with grooming and exploitation against a backdrop of poverty, widening inequality and a lack of alternative opportunities for these young people. This overlap between victim, offender and conscious choice presents challenges in the current response, where there can be a binary approach in categorising individuals either as victims or perpetrators.'

But what seemed clear was that these children were, and are, the missing. Positioned somewhere underneath the radar of mainstream society, sometimes without anyone searching at all. It reminded me of what Ann Coffey had said about children in care. It wasn't that people weren't aware of this fairly recent development in the UK's ever more volatile drug markets. It's just that many didn't have the resources or know-how to deal with it. Going missing is made much easier when there's no one tracking you down. For many of the thousands of children going country, their lives were already filled with precarity. They might have been kicked out of mainstream education or be living in chaotic households, or – like the 15-year-old boy maimed many miles from his London home – failed by ever more stretched local authorities, whose youth services have been stripped to the bone. The stresses of their new lives poised between home and whatever town they soon happen to find themselves in. Threat levels are high, as Max had explained. Rivals gangs, desperate users, their manipulative, violent bosses. Some will even ask their parents not to report them as missing to avoid any more untoward attention – while others wouldn't agree with the idea of being missing at all. There is also a racial element to all this, with the NCA's missing figures showing that black children – representing the majority of those going country – are more than three times more likely to go missing than their white peers. And what, I needed to know, happened when they did come home, just as most of the missing do until they end up leaving again. What was being put in place to help stop this revolving door of vulnerable children pinballing between being in and out of vision?

The Children's Society is one of the UK's best-known children's charities which has spent the last few years developing their Disrupting Exploitation programme, working with police, local authorities, schools and the NHS. Much of their attention is on county lines. Becky Fedia is the programme's National Project Manager, a role she started in the first months of 2020. When we spoke, she was already a couple of months in situ and things were just as manically busy as ever, she explained with a smile. It's a big role, with teams in London, Birmingham and Manchester. Their work sees them interact with local partners in each city, ranging from social work to police and education partnerships. 'It's about changing problematic contexts and procedures around children that mean they aren't getting the support that they need.' One example Becky brought up was their work with the Met Police in London, looking at the point of arrest for young people found with drugs. 'What does that procedure look like? How can we turn that from a point of criminalisation to one of recognising that this is a young person that needs support?'

'Lots of the young people we work with go missing,' Becky explained to me. 'It's great working with them and working with them in their own circumstances. But I guess the whole point of the project is disrupting it so that when another young person comes along they have a different experience of the system and don't come across the same barriers.' The question for Becky and her colleagues was how could they improve these systems so that the same thing doesn't just repeat itself, again and again. After being approached by the Met, they helped revamp their interactions in custody with the young people they'd arrest, whose existing experiences with law enforcement tended to be hostile. 'The police example is a really good one. We agreed a plan of work with them where our staff would go in and do observations and just watch everything that happened.' It ended in a list of recommendations, which ranged from things as basic as offering a young person a drink that wasn't tea or coffee, all the way up to missed opportunities for safeguarding referrals. 'If that young person has been arrested with £2000 in cash on them and it's been confiscated, what does it mean for them once they've been released? Who are they now in debt to? There needs to be a safety plan for when they're back in the community.' The recommendations grew into a full training programme, which had seen over 1000 of the force's custody staff benefit from. '[It's about] thinking about that moment as one where you can put a stopper on what is happening with that young person,' Becky added. It's by no means a finished process, she said, but an ongoing piece of work. Just one example of the 'many, many times we've jumped in where an opportunity is being missed'. It's a potential moment of intervention. 'From our perspective, we can't [physically] stop a person going missing. Maybe this is controversial, but what we can do is make sure they're as safe as possible. Are you telling somebody where you are? Are you keeping your phone charged? Do you have numbers of people you can call in an emergency? Do you have cash on you? Is there any way they can maintain contact? We have to appreciate that very often we don't know what happens when a young person has gone missing [this way].' It depends how much is known about the young person's situation, which isn't always a lot. 'If the perpetrator is present with them, then how can they keep that number hidden in a safe way? It depends on the circumstance, but it's safety planning with an understanding that that young person has to lead that process as they know what's going on much better than we do.'

Return interviews are one means of understanding exactly what has happened to a missing young person. They are a statutory requirement for any child who has run away, or disappeared from care or their family home. In the best-case scenario, it should be led by an independent professional who the returned child trusts, though this is often easier said than done. It is a chance to understand what has happened and to identify the risk of it happening again. Where did you go? What harm might have occurred? It isn't an interrogation, or shouldn't be at any rate. The point isn't to judge, but to work towards something like understanding. After initial contact, there will be a first meeting. It might take place at home or in another suitable, non-threatening location. The Children's Society guidance is clear. Turn up on time, don't be surprised if they have forgotten the meeting or don't particularly want to talk. Persistence is important, but not to the point of hectoring the young person who has returned from the missing episode. The interviewer needs to be able to pick up on potential risk factors and communicate in a way that isn't an adult's conception of what is and isn't a missing child. Becky told me how 'pretty much none of the young people would recognise themselves as victims of exploitation or as a missing young person. I don't think I've ever heard that before. That's sometimes where services run into issues because they'll try and engage a young person on that level. That's not the young person's life. My background is in frontline work and I can honestly say I've never heard them [express themselves] as missing.'

We were back again at the question of what makes a missing person. In the adult world of services, law enforcement and distraught parents, these were missing children. For the young people themselves it was more complex than that. In their world, with its intricacies so unknowable to the adults on the other side of the divide, it was just the day-to-day reality of their lives. How could you be missing from something you seemed to be in the centre of?

The more I delved into the things that drove people into disappearance, the more clouded the picture grew. The homelessness crisis had led into addiction, which had led into the subterranean world of the taken and modern slavery, which had in term led into the crumbling system of children's homes and the explosive rise of county lines, a social evil with clearly potted roots and no magical formula to cure it. Much had started to connect in my tour through the missing. What linked Crisis at Christmas to Eagle's Wings Trust and the missing teenagers selling crack and heroin far from home in decaying seaside towns across the country? Poverty, starved services, the erosion of the already imperfect social safety net that used to catch people before they fell out of vision. The wider the canvas became, the more clearly I was beginning to see Christobal in my mind. Or maybe that wasn't quite right. Though his figure loomed increasingly large with every development, the edges around him were still blurred. But the more I learned of the missing, the more sense his story was starting to make. Though perhaps that wasn't it either – not exactly. My mind had been working at double speed, trying to process the stories of the people I had encountered in the context of my own past, though there was still something unsaid, lurking underneath the surface. There were a few nights when I dreamt of Spain and La Línea, or at least the childish, primary-coloured approximation of it that I half-remembered. It was if there was a silent force behind my steps, pushing in the direction of a place that was still so unfamiliar to me, on almost every level.

It was time for the next stage in my journey through the missing. Talk of the statutory return interviews had sparked something else in me. If I'd seen something of the places that people were disappearing into, I wanted to understand what it meant to come home.

PART IV
THE RETURNING MISSING

CHAPTER 9

Esther Beadle closed the front door and walked out of her life at 10 p.m. on Friday, 29 January 2016. She was seen leaving her shared house in Cowley, a bustling neighbourhood about an hour's walk from the centre of Oxford. At that moment, she was in vision. Then she was gone. For the next 41 hours, Esther was a missing person in the eyes of the law, the media and her loved ones. Alarm bells had started to ring on the Saturday, when she hadn't turned up to a social call in London. The sudden disappearance was out of character for the then 27-year-old, according to a tweet posted by the friend she'd been supposed to meet.

On its surface, Esther's life wasn't that of someone at risk of vanishing. She had a flourishing career as assistant news editor at the *Oxford Mail*, a job she loved and had worked hard to get. There was never any question, Esther was good at what she did. From a difficult upbringing in Newcastle, she'd trained as a journalist in her home city and moved a few hundred miles up the north-east coast to Aberdeen in 2012, where she'd spent a couple of years learning her trade as a reporter for a busy daily paper in the city, covering everything from child poverty to families separated by visa issues. Those years weren't just marked by success. Not everything was as controlled and orderly as work, where her editors only ever had praise for her clean copy and consistently punchy stories. Her childhood and adolescence had been marked by domestic abuse and deep-seated traumas that had never been adequately treated or addressed.

There was a point in those years when Esther had realised she was an alcoholic. There was no other way of putting it. The early shift would end at 2 p.m. and a bottle of wine would quickly turn to two, would turn to pints at the pub and a bottle of gin back at home until she passed out. Gradually, with the help of supportive editorial colleagues and counselling, things started to ease and improve. By April 2014, she had moved south, to start at the *Oxford Mail*, helping to run the newsroom, managing reporters and tending to the daily whirlwind of work at a major regional newspaper. It was the life she had wanted. Professional status and a new city that was starting to feel like home, as well as a stable relationship with the man she hoped to build her future with. But there was something else, something nameless under the superficial calm and order. And on that night in late January, it had surfaced. She hadn't planned to become a missing person, whatever that meant. It was just that one minute she was somewhere she was supposed to be, the next she was somewhere else. After taking £150 out of a cashpoint, Esther made her way to London, where she'd already made a reservation at a hotel. The next couple of days were a blur of impressions and ordeals, as well as ever escalating concern from her loved ones.

There was a second central London hotel that Sunday, a Travelodge, and an attempt to further insulate herself from the outside world. It was a plan that made total sense to her then. It was also when Esther started to understand what was going on online. The Saturday had seen a trickle of posts across social media, but it was quickly becoming a flood. She was everywhere she looked, amplified across Facebook and Twitter. Her name, her face, her personal details plastered across the UK and beyond. Have you seen this woman? Red hair, glasses and a strong Geordie accent: an entire existence stripped down to bullet points. Every hour, things were snowballing. Here she was, somewhere outside of her life in a nondescript London hotel. She was meant to be alone, but it wasn't what solitude was supposed to feel like. Her phone was deluged with increasingly panicked messages and phone calls, from family and relative strangers, up to and including her Year 9 geography teacher. Esther couldn't bring herself to answer them. This wasn't the solitude she was searching for. Then there were the actual strangers. People inserting themselves into her private messages, asking where she'd gone and when she was coming back. Going out by herself was difficult as the police were searching after her report had been sent to the

Met. The press were involved now, with online news stories starting to circulate. Esther didn't really have a plan and the more hours that passed, the clearer it became that the outside world wasn't going to melt away. On the late afternoon of Sunday, 31 January, she walked into St Thomas's Hospital, a few yards from the crowds of tourists on Westminster Bridge and asked to see the mental health crisis team. Esther's missing episode, as the rest of the world seemed to be calling it, was over. She had been found 'safe and well' to use the standard jargon tacked on to the people who come back alive and physically unscathed. Esther was back in sight, but the story of her return had barely begun.

It's the way it often goes. Of the 180,000 reported missing every year in the UK, most do return in one way or another. Like Esther, they vanish for a few days at a time to take a step outside of whatever might be going in their lives. It's what would have applied to Christobal back in the mid-1990s, during the fractious point in his and Mum's relationship when I was still little more than a toddler, when he would leave and return as his mood or circumstances dictated. I'd read the stats right at the beginning of my reporting, the figures that show how over a third of all reported incidents are repeat incidents: the people pinballing between being here and somewhere else. Around 97 per cent of missing people either come home or are found dead within a week. Within a year, that figure climbs to 99 per cent.[23] After the months trying to understand where people went, I wanted to know what happened when they came back. Yet the more I dug in, the less sense it made. To return seemed to be an act coated in silence. Official support for returning adults in the UK appeared meagre to the point of non-existence, lacking even the flawed framework I'd seen in place for children when talking to Becky at The Children's Society, or with former MP Ann Coffey. When I first came across Esther's story in the spring of 2019, I knew I had to speak with her. This wasn't an abstract academic or professional question we were talking about. This was her life: it hadn't been lived by anyone else. She, along with thousands upon thousands of others every year, had come back from a state that isn't easy to define and could offer a unique insight into what it meant. Esther had been missing, but that wasn't the whole of it. Her story seemed to encompass much of what I'd already encountered, from London to Manchester, and what I'd learned or thought I understood of Christobal. Strained services colliding with the patchwork of circumstances that lead to lives gradually slipping, from control to something else. How it doesn't ever seem to happen all at once.

I'd been looking forward to meeting Esther from when we'd first followed each other on Twitter after my first missing feature was published, right through to late summer in 2020 when we finally met in a pub on the Quayside in Newcastle, a few weeks after my first visit on the way to Dundee to visit Eagles Wings Trust. We'd exchanged messages over the months and a few plans to meet had been cancelled or rearranged as other bits of life managed to plant themselves in the way. Finally, a convenient day presented itself on the August Bank Holiday weekend. The train journey up had melted past, from a deserted early morning King's Cross to an equally quiet Newcastle city centre. Walking down Northumberland Street, it didn't feel much like a Saturday afternoon in the embers of August. There was a heavy Sunday feeling layered over everything, from the half-empty shops to the old man pubs with a few desultory smokers outside, who looked glued there from habit rather than anything resembling pleasure. It didn't matter too much. There were a couple of hours before we were due to meet, so I dragged myself up and down a few familiar walks that I'd gleaned from my previous trip, as the sky kept turning in and out of itself, from clusters of ominous dark clouds to a few glimpses of weak sunshine through the predominant heavy grey.

There's a feeling that never quite became normal in reporting this book and one I was often sheepish to admit to – the odd sense of intrusion that sometimes came before a long-anticipated interview. Yes, Esther had spoken about her experiences before in an academic setting as well as collaborating on a short piece in the *Daily Record*, the Scottish tabloid newspaper, in 2018. But this was different. It was me asking questions that she might not want to answer, ground she had covered so many times already, both to others and within herself. As I wolfed down lunch and looked over my notes, I could feel a few pangs of nerves, attributable to too much cheap coffee as much as anything else.

We'd agreed to meet at 3.30 p.m. at Head of Steam, a pub tucked down a side street from the waterfront. She'd arrived just before me, she said, as I joined her at a table outside. At first, we made a bit of small talk about our 2020 attempts to quit smoking. Esther was well ahead of me, having stopped a few weeks before and hadn't touched a cigarette since. I offered sincere, slightly envious congratulations as I rifled around my pockets for a filter and Esther popped another piece of nicotine gum. Things were ok, she told me, in a year that had already been as odd for her as it had been for everyone else during the pandemic. Esther has been teaching journalism master's students for the last couple of years at Newcastle University, part of an online journalism module in their wider studies. It's work she enjoys, even if she sometimes misses the buzz of the newsroom. From the minute I sat down we fell into conversation naturally, with the pre-interview anxiety melting away in minutes. I don't suppose it was a surprise to see she still had the experienced journalist's skill of putting people at ease.

Not long into our talk, Esther made something clear. There's no easy answer to why she decided to do what she did and go where she went. True, she'd long dealt with fragile mental health. It's a common thread that connects the missing, as both a cause and consequence. For those 41 hours, she had been part of the statistic that shows approximately 80 per cent of all missing adults in the UK are thought to be living with some form of mental illness. In Esther's undergraduate days there had been a long and severe battle with clinical depression, but that wasn't it. In 2016, after her return, she was diagnosed with borderline personality disorder, a condition that carries more than its fair amount of stigma and misunderstanding. It might explain some of how she felt and the tone of some of her actions then. On the Friday of her disappearance, there were signs of what Esther now considers to be hypomania, a common hallmark of BPD. Everything in the build-up to walking out was instinctual, to the point of being 'almost feral', she explained to me. Something told her she would need cash and not her debit card. 'I took that money out of the cashpoint, which I'd never do normally but I knew that I didn't want anybody to know where I was going. I just [knew] I wanted to be away. Away from existence, I suppose. I booked a hotel on Expedia while I sat in my living room, chatting to my housemate telling them everything was fine, that I was going to be fine. In hindsight, [it] was manic.' After checking herself into hospital on the Sunday, she told a sympathetic psychiatrist who didn't quite believe it when Esther had mentioned the press interest in her case. 'She came back 15 minutes later white as a sheet.' The police turned up a few hours later, though the two officers didn't sit down or introduce themselves, aside from the most basic questions. Had she been a victim of crime when she had been away, they asked disinterestedly. It was hard to answer, Esther told me, as 'I was away with the pixies, banging my head on the wall'.

The few weeks after her return to Oxford still carry a feeling of unreality. Everything had started to unravel so fast. Esther has been back in Newcastle since the early spring of 2016, about six weeks after her return. It wasn't the kind of homecoming she'd ever envisaged. The emotional and personal fallout from her 'missing episode' had been profound, a series of dominos that fell in rapid succession as personal relationships fell under strain, and resuming fast-paced professional life proved impossible. 'Within those six weeks of being returned, I'd lost my house, my job, my partner, the city I'd started to call home. And I came back to where I didn't really have a home. I couldn't move in with my mum or dad, so I ended up with an aunty for about nine months as I sort of got back into society.' People started treating her differently. Her family, understandably worried, didn't want her to go on a camping trip even months later, which felt odd after a lifetime of independence. It could be tiresome, 'as you can't just get up and go. [That] lasted a long time, particularly with my family. It's odd, as after the age of about 11 it had been "off you pop".' Official support was almost non-existent, though she still speaks highly of colleagues at the paper who 'who were absolutely brilliant', she told me. It was just as well, as there was nothing from the police or any other body to help her navigate life post-missing, as strange as that term still felt. There was nothing at all to help her understand the dislocation she'd just lived through, no return interview or concerted effort to make sure it didn't happen again. After moving back to Newcastle, it took Esther the best part of a year to get anything like the kind of professional mental health support she needed. 'They'd been really good on the Oxford side and faxed everything over. I turned up to the GP in Newcastle and they were absolutely fantastic. After that it was different. I ended up going pillar to post for nine months, shunted around different services. I'd gone from very intensive support to nothing. I'd spend up until 4 p.m. in bed and struggle to put my shoes on when I did.'

It was hard to talk to people about what had happened. Worried loved ones, her old housemates, the random woman in the street who stopped her to say how happy she was that Esther was home. It's like there just wasn't the right language there to address the subject in hand. I told her I sometimes felt something similar about Christobal. If he was dead, like Mum, then it would be easier. Not missing to me or from me, lost somewhere in a kind of permanent vagueness. With her professional background, it seemed natural to Esther to want to dive into missing, to try and work through some of what happened to her and understand statistics that showed 'how it's like a city the size of Stoke goes missing every year'. Not too long after her return, she'd started on some work with Missing People, speaking at events and academic conferences. Sometimes it felt worthwhile, '[though it could also feel] like I was being put forward as a token returned missing person, rather than that it being co-productional,' she told me, though she still spoke highly of the charity.

Over the course of 2020, I'd noticed how small and closely related the professional world of the missing is in the UK. As Esther and I spoke, the same names kept recurring, the gallery of academics and police officers we both knew or whose research we were familiar with, from across the UK. There was Joe Apps in London and Dr Penny Woolnough at Abertay University in Dundee, who I hadn't met but knew from her work on the returning missing. It could often feel like everyone knew everyone else. Interviews would begin and end with enthusiastic recommendations of people I might find it interesting to speak to. Before long into mine and Esther's conversation, another familiar name cropped up.

Professor Hester Parr is based at Glasgow University and is a distinguished geographer and one of the UK's leading experts on missing people. Back in February 2020, we'd met for a coffee at her office, tucked up in one of the university's picturesque quadrangles. It was a crisp, bright morning as I jostled my way through packs of groggy students on their way to or from their early lectures. A few weeks before, I'd read through *Geographies of Missing*, a 2013 research project run from Glasgow, in collaboration with Dundee University and Police Scotland. Hester was one of its authors, along with Penny Woolnough and two other academics, Olivia Stevenson and Nick Fyfe. It's a powerful body of work, light in academic jargon and full of considered, deeply human stories about missing experience, to help police better their response to the returned. 'Our intervention was to try and bring these stories back and make it seem like people,' Hester had explained to me that winter morning. 'To build empathy and emotional connections. Feedback was dead positive.' But she wasn't alone in feeling the piecemeal responses weren't enough. 'I still felt the big thing was a sector-level response on what to do [when people return]. If you have so many thousands continually going missing, surely something needs to be done to prevent that. What do you do with an adult missing person when they come back? The police would basically do the safe-and-well check. "Are you alright, did anything happen, were you harmed? Ok, on you go back home." Our message around that was that it wasn't good enough.' To Hester, it doesn't mean simply pointing the finger at police forces alone. '[This should] be a demand on our entire society to come up with different responses to that moment, which should be a moment of prevention and intervention. There needs to be multiple professions involved in this, not just the police. Health services, social work, local authorities. We need to start a national conversation on the return.'

It's been something of a personal mission for Hester over the years, involving much collaboration with fellow academics and various other professions. 'The project [started] in partnership with the police. At that time, Penny Woolnough was a police researcher and she was our contact. They had a lot of information about a certain kind of profile of a certain kind of missing person and the distance they would go. We knew where people started and ended up, but our job was to fill in the gaps.' It was about collecting stories that spoke of more than just raw data, Hester added. 'We engaged some of the 99 per cent of people who come back in an interview situation, a bit like this. Asking more about their journey.' Not just what made them leave, though that came into it. Instead, it was how they had used their environment, how they made decisions when they were away, how long they were away. 'Literally, where do you go? These weren't people that were homeless. Actually, they led pretty average lives until something snapped,' Hester said with an illustrative click of her fingers. For those who do leave without existing networks, without being used to the street and how to navigate it, how best to survive going missing? As well as Esther, I thought of David and the others that I'd met at Crisis at Christmas or the rough sleepers Hendrix and Hannah had spoken about at Coffee4Craig. Those who had either just arrived at life on the streets or were perilously close to it. The impossibility of preparing for the first time, not knowing what it is that you're stepping into. The missing were the same, I thought. Stepping out seemed to be the easy part. Knowing what to do after was another matter.

My conversation with Hester in Glasgow had thrown up another tension, one that Esther knew well from her own experience. The fear of being looked for set against the feeling of wanting to be found. There are many who don't trust the police, or any kind of authority, for all sorts of reasons. After exchanging goodbyes with Hester, I'd reread part of *Geographies of Missing*, a section titled 'Missing People, Missing Voices: Stories of Missing Experience', in a cafe in Glasgow's West End. Sorted into neat sections, each showcasing a different type of missing episode, it speaks entirely in the voices of the missing themselves. They range from Sophie's story, which outlines what it was like to be missing for 24 hours, up to Andrew's, detailing his month-long absence. Each tale is moving in its immediacy. Here were the missing in their own words, centred at the heart of their own experience. One account, Peter's, details what it felt like being missing and subsequently located by the police. His journey had begun after leaving home with his passport and driving licence, to keep his options open. The reasons for his flight aren't made explicit. Peter wasn't thinking straight. He was desperate and it almost felt like he was being chased. Peter was frightened about being stopped by law enforcement, so he kept moving to get as far away as possible, trying to conjure up a plan just as Esther had done. After arriving in Leicester, he'd thrown his phone away in panic. Peter's mistrust of the police stemmed from a run-in as a younger man 'at a drunk and stupid age', in his words. After two days of aimless meandering around the city, he was walking up a side road when a car sidled up, its headlights blaring at full beam. The driver came out and asked if Peter was alright, to which he responded, 'Yes and no'. The man was a police officer, working with a partner. They were both young and jovial. But Peter was beside himself, not knowing what the consequences of 'going missing' might hold. He panicked, crying for them not to take him away, that he hadn't done anything wrong. 'You have to come with us,' the officers said. They were kind, Peter recalls. Making a few jokes and trying to lighten the mood as they calmed him down. They asked questions. Have you ever been suicidal? How did you get here? Did you get your money from the bank? How do you feel? They were broadly sympathetic, unlike Esther's responding officer. No one told Peter he was a bad person or that he shouldn't have run away. But once he'd settled down, the thought of the return started to play on his mind. The idea of going home was wrapped in fear – though the reasons are left deliberately ambiguous. Peter would have preferred to have stayed away for longer and didn't feel as if he was 'strong enough' to go back. He was 'depressed and out of it' and even though the individual policemen had treated him with dignity, their involvement ended almost as soon as it had started. He had been found, case closed. Peter still had to return, without having had the chance to wrap his head around why he had gone missing in the first place, with no likely support forthcoming to help him understand. The section ends with him 'still [feeling] confused about what happened to me', still grappling for meaning and a cohesive explanation of his journey.

It felt like everywhere I turned there were those who could offer a cogent diagnosis of the failures facing the returning missing. All the kinds of support that were desperately needed and overdue. Esther herself has advocated for the introduction of formal return interviews, across the UK, to make the most of that critical moment of prevention and intervention that Hester had described to me in Glasgow. Back then, Hester and I had spoken for an hour or so by the time we reached her work on the National Missing Persons Framework for Scotland, which had launched in 2017 after years of what felt like endless conversations and technical refinement. Commissioned by the Scottish government, it linked together the police, the NHS, housing charities and a number of other third-sector organisations. Progress could be glacial, Hester had explained to me. 'I turned up to committee meetings for three years and discussed the same things. That's the slight frustration about government processes. Then nothing happened and all the staff changed. It got to the point where I said – and as an academic I can say what I like really – look it's never going to be perfect but you just need to get some guidance out there,' she'd added. 'It now means there is guidance in Scotland with a big emphasis on return. There is now a commitment by Police Scotland to have "return discussions", as they are called, with everyone who goes missing. And it is a commitment, even if there is still work to do.' One suggestion is that these interviews could work best if they weren't conducted by police at all. 'Other agencies should be doing it, which does happen in other parts of Scotland and I think England as well, where bits of interview work is contracted out. Places like Barnardo's or another charity who might be better placed to handle that kind of conversation. Someone non-threatening.'

'There's something really basic here,' Hester had added. 'When someone goes missing, they've been traumatised by something and the only response is to go, to just disappear. They're walking around trying to manage this and the least we can do is to talk to that person who has come back and ask what happened. And not just what happened, but a discussion [around it]. That means referral, whether that's a GP or a community mental health team. It really comes to having adequate mental health services in our society.' It made me think of the stories I'd encountered of the teenagers who had returned from going country, only to rub against indifferent or ill-trained officers who compounded the existing trauma. Or those like Esther, who had returned but subsequently struggled to access the services they needed. Though Scotland might be slightly ahead of the rest of the UK, it doesn't mean there's any room for complacency. The work has to be continual: training people to train other people, across professions. 'Scotland is leading the way a little bit, though there's still tonnes of work to do,' Hester had said. 'Missing people are one of these really difficult social problems that doesn't just have one solution. It requires so many people working together. One of the answers is to have multi-agency groups that have missing as part of their agenda. If that was mandated across the UK then you'd see some improvement, because people have to talk to each other.' Over the long months of reporting, it was constantly hammered home to me just how key communication is to keeping people in vision: the missing and returned, as well as those who repeatedly slip between the two states. Hester had been keen to stress that the missing are not the other. 'It's not like missing people are some weird separate group that are floating about. It's us. We are the future missing people. It could happen to me or you. Services are stretched, but I don't think [missing] was on the agenda before.' The new framework has seen some big improvements, even if the picture is inevitably mixed. In September 2020, a group chaired by Hester published a report on its implementation, having been asked by Ash Denham, Scotland's Minister for Community Safety. Of the group's key recommendations, there is the need for continued funding and development, with no room to stand still on the progress already made.

Months after my visit to Glasgow, the late summer afternoon in Newcastle was drifting into evening as Esther explained to me how coming across Hester's and the others' work had been an important milestone after her own return. Here was something that chimed with her own experiences in a way that felt like being spoken, rather than dictated, to. Though it still seemed odd to think *Geographies of Missing* remains quite so much of an anomaly even all these years on from publication. '[It's still] pretty unique, but it was old even when I was studying it two or three years ago. But it was fantastic to me to read. Just little words and phrases that are in it, from people who had very different missing experiences to mine. Every so often, I'd be reading and think, yes – that connects. The language is so important.' We returned to the question of the police. Back when Esther spoke at academic conferences on missing, the responses could vary. It was interesting, she explained to me, to see how the police in the crowd responded to one of her addresses. 'It wasn't like I went up on stage and blasted [them]. I'd said, "This is what happened to me and this is what I feel needs to happen", from my perspective. When it came time for questions, you could see the coppers in the audience thinking, "She's stood up there saying we don't do anything [to help the missing]", and obviously felt quite personally affronted by it. It was more that just a business card might be useful? Because I'd had literally nothing.'

There was something else I'd wanted to ask Esther. One of the most striking parts of *Geographies of Missing* is how it tracks the contours of the journey itself. Most of the interviewees spoke about trips by train, or bus, or even foot that ended somewhere familiar. The process might have been fraught: for every degree of planning there is another of panic. Usually, the destination is somewhere they once lived or worked. Perhaps they still had friends or relatives in the area. Going missing is not always the same as being lost. It made me think of Christobal's movements, from London back to La Línea, his true home. In Esther's case, it wasn't an accident that one of the first things she did on the Saturday after going off-grid was to take herself to the

South Bank. It's strange, the way you find yourself drawn to places. She'd been to university at King's College, right on the Strand. It felt so normal, sitting in the sunshine with a coffee and a pain au chocolat, watching the world drift by. The next purchase was a notebook and pen. 'The rest of the day, I sat and wrote. It was all I could do because I thought "that's what I do". I'm a writer. I wrote pages and pages over the course of that day, to set down whatever it was that was in my head. It's a really interesting thing, to see where I was and what I was feeling, almost like a log, which isn't something many other people [with the same experience] might have.' Even with that record, it still occasionally feels like that weekend was something that happened to someone else, in a time and place at once familiar and almost absurdly remote. I asked her if it felt like an interregnum, an invisible dividing line between the person she was then and the person sitting in front of me, that afternoon in Newcastle. 'It does feel for me, and having spoken to a couple of other returned missing people, that life is very much divided into before and after. I think that would probably apply to everyone who has been touched by missing. People like yourself who have missing loved ones, as well as people who have gone missing [themselves].' Naturally, there are times when she grieves for what might have been, if she hadn't walked out the door that night, though these thoughts don't consume her. I told her I often felt the same, trapped with the thoughts of a life full of different choices. But things are far better now than they were then. 'It's still the traumatic thing I've been through. I was thinking this morning if I'd still call it that and, yes, it is,' Esther said. '[But] I'm very healthy, happy and secure in myself [now] and very pleased I'm back in Newcastle, where I've met amazing people. If it all hadn't happened then I wouldn't be here now. I wouldn't have the partner I have and I wouldn't have the mental health bits and pieces that I do, now.'

Living with BPD means many different things for Esther. Identity is crucial, her sense of who she is and the place she inhabits in the world. It might have seemed like a small act, but buying that notebook that Saturday afternoon was a link back to what she thought she knew about herself. 'I thought that writing, journaling, having things down on paper, was some sort of anchor,' she added. Perhaps it also served as some small proof of her wanting to return at some point, rather than disappear permanently. 'There's a bit of me that thinks, well, I must have wanted to stay because – pardon the brusqueness of what I'm about to say – I didn't just throw myself in front of a tube train, which did go through my mind. I was convinced I was going to die, that it was the end. Not even just the end of my life, but some kind of existential ending. I was sure that I'd be dead by the end of that Saturday, whether it was getting knocked down by a bus or going in front of a train, or going into the Thames. I was waiting for it to happen rather than actively seeking it out. It was when it got to midnight on the Saturday, that's when I started to panic.

Things hadn't gone the way I thought they were going to go.'

Esther isn't alone in identifying the complexity of what's at stake: the vast spectrum of experience that missing covers. I'd heard it from Joe and Kirsty at Missing People, as well as Tony up in Dundee. We were back at that question again, the one it still seemed impossible to shake or solve. What is a missing person and what does it mean, as a label applied to an individual life? Early on in our conversation, Esther had raised a point that struck at the heart of it. Perspective matters, she explained. Understanding that was crucial for herself and others. 'In my own experience, I didn't see myself as a missing person. Stuff happened to me. I was there, inside it. To everybody else, I was a missing person. But in my eyes, they were missing from me. I'd removed myself from everything else that had been going on, to try and push the world away.' So much emphasis, she continued, is usually placed on what happens to everybody else but the missing person, 'who is in this vacuum of support and, potentially, reality. That's what may have happened to me. I've never spoken about my missing episode in any kind of therapeutic environment. Instead, I've only ever gone on conference stages and relayed it.' Even four and a half years on, she isn't quite sure how to explain what happened over that weekend, when she walked outside of everything. How to sum it up, to solve the question of agency at its root. 'Is it what I did, or what happened to me? I can't quite place myself in that. It might be that it's a mixture of both.'

After leaving Esther, I had an hour or so to kill until the train back to London. There wasn't enough time for anything much, aside from a hasty trip to WH Smith before settling down to the three and a half hours south, barrelling down the coast as the evening faded into dark. It had been a long day of travel and I was glad to be on my way home again. My partner had texted to say she'd be out at a friend's place by the time I arrived back at King's Cross, so I treated myself to the slow, almost entirely empty 63 bus home. My legs had stiffened and my back felt like it belonged to someone else by the time it arrived back in Peckham and I stood at the Nigel Road stop waiting for my connection to Nunhead. Saturday night and I'd never seen the streets so empty of everything. None of the usual well-to-do revellers making their way loudly from bar to bar and none of the regular faces who walk the same streets day and night asking for a bit of spare change for a hostel or something to eat. Thoughts of the returning missing kept coming to me as I walked the last few minutes home in the deserted, half-suburban roads. Home, that's where I was going. Somewhere safe and warm that I could call my own. How many were out there that night, I wondered, who had just left or were on the precipice of a return, who didn't have anything like the same privilege of stability? To me, turning the key in the lock of an empty flat was the simplest thing in the world. I'd started to learn that for so many others coming back just offered the same uncertainty and pain as going away from it all in the first place. Having unpacked, I turned on the TV and tried to clear the missing out of my head for a few hours, if only to ward off the spectre of another sleepless night.

CHAPTER 10

Mum's funeral had been the first I ever attended, a simple enough service and cremation at Honor Oak Crematorium in the early autumn of 1999. Truthfully, I can remember very little of the occasion outside of a procession of imposing adults in black and an almost leaden atmosphere; of something oppressive and clammy in the air. The most vivid memory is that my friend Charlie was there to keep me company, and how we spent most of the morning managing to fall into mischief by wandering into the forbidden parts of the grounds. Later, when trying to piece the day together for the benefit of my adolescent self, I found out that during the service someone read one of Christina Rossetti's most famous poems, 'Remember', a favourite of Mum's. It ends with a memorable injunction from a voice beyond the grave, talking back to its living loved ones and concluding that it might always be better by far you should forget and smile than that you should remember and be sad.

Since that morning I must have attended another ten funerals, or thereabouts. Some have been shows of solidarity with a friend. Others have been for my own close family and occasionally friends. I have served as a pallbearer and written eulogies I've eventually been too daunted to deliver myself. But mostly I have tried to follow the example of others, by sitting quietly in slightly too large suits, eyes bowed with respectful hurt. Perhaps it's strange, how quickly you get used to the squashed intensity of the days themselves and their rituals.

In June 2009, my grandmother, Nancy, died, a few months short of a decade on from Mum. In the years between, we had shared so much. We had lived together for the previous decade in our unconventional little family unit, her, myself and my aunt. Gran's long life had been full of as much good and ill as you might expect from someone who had made it to 86 in mostly high spirits. What I remember from her cremation and service is a jumble of a different kind. The officiating humanist celebrant traced the narrative thread of her life with a practised skill. From her rootless Australian upbringing, through to her wild early days as a journalist in London in the golden age of Fleet Street, followed by marriage, the arrival of children and the big move to suburbia. How the idyll soon chafed and the marriage broke down. The return to London and the peripatetic years of poverty and constant crisscrossing of the city, from flat to flat, job to job. Her eventual settling in Catford, the arrival of grandchildren and the harsh years after my mum, her daughter's, death. Then, the final golden years, spent back and forth from Scottish suburbia and the flat on Faversham Road. Her wit and occasionally over-bearing kindness, her relentless curiosity and refusal to treat anything important with any importance for too long, lest it might become permanent. The highlights reel of an entire life, all of it, distilled down into a 15-minute compilation, read by a stranger in a dismal, oak-panelled room.

It felt impossible to cry at something so professional and smooth, an occurrence so blatantly fringed with unreality. After the ceremony, there was the wake. I doubt I'll ever forget my friend Matthew coming up to me with some comforting words. 'I'd no idea about all the things she'd done,' he told me quietly. I wondered then, as I wonder still, if you'd even recognise your own life delivered as a eulogy? All of the idiosyncrasies and nothing days and years condensed to smoothness, to a somehow comprehensible straight line from birth to death. The turnout had been good, she was a well-loved woman, capable of inspiring many devoted friendships, some spanning many decades. Did her companions from the old days, both careless and careworn, recognise the portrait of her? The celebrant, a thin and almost stiflingly respectable man, didn't touch on the complicated relationship she had shared with my mum and, by extension, Christobal. I suppose it wasn't the time or place, as these pages have the capacity to be.

Gran was more than capable of an all-intensive love. She often thought nothing of giving out everything she had, at a moment's notice. All the traits that made her an unim-peachable grandmother could make her a difficult woman in the myriad other facets of her life. It was often remarked with a smile how she could grudge and row with the best of them. Her relationship with Mum, her middle daughter, could sometimes be fraught. For the years of Mum's late adolescence and early 20s, they lived together in a succession of small flats around London. Times were hard and a combination of poverty and proximity could spell difficulties. Too much of either can be a potent thing in any relationship, no matter how much love is involved. But you had to laugh, most of the time. After one blazing row between them Gran had thrown a handful of half-cooked sausages from the oven to the floor, a scene so wildly melodramatic that it instantly became a part of family folklore, still laughingly repeated decades later. She always had a habit of building food into her voluminous stories, as both a marker of someone's character or occasionally even a fully fledged supporting character in its own right.

Her and Christobal's relationship had started off fine. She approved of his match with her daughter. His suitability was never the issue. At first, things were as well as they possibly could be, material circumstances permitting. The three of them squeezed into her already cramped flat could be claustrophobic, but what alternative was there? She was fond of him and, I imagine, happy to fuss over a young man she sensed probably needed it. It was only when things started to turn in his life, at the point where his behaviour was starting to cause Mum pain, that Gran's opinion of her son-in-law started to shift. Family could be a case of us against them to her. If you hurt one of hers, that might well be it. Much later, when it was just the two of us she would sometimes remark to me about Christobal with sadness and regret. How he was a good enough man, but too silly or scared to do the right thing. Naturally, being Gran, she would always end her recollections half-dissolving into laughter with the lament that it was such a shame, as 'he'd made such a good rice pudding'. We didn't really talk about him all that much. Life just seemed so full of other things to enjoy.

Even in the truculent depths of my teenage years, we'd talk about the books and writers she loved, from Siegfried Sassoon to Anthony Hecht. Though it was hard for her to read, in those last years, now Mum was dead. Anything new was too painful, she'd tell me, and we'd usually leave it at that. Soon, when I started to fully shed the last vestiges of adolescent embarrassment and let my enthusiasm run unchecked, we'd spend hours discussing her old favourites, which were still so fresh and new to me then. Even in the final few months, when her mind would wander to unlit places, there would be moments of perfect clarity. Some snatch of song or verse would be recalled and spark a few minutes of calm. We'd use them to talk, or else just enjoy the companionable peace and silence, the two of us briefly sitting on the same page again. I like to think that she'd have loved the direction my life was taking, if she was still here to see it. That she'd have been thrilled to see another journalist in the family, resurrecting the old traditions after a generation's remove. But I also know without question that she'd have been proud whatever I'd chosen to do, or had forced on me by circumstance. Her pride in me was entirely unconditional, as it was for the rest of her family.

It's tough to say when the summer of 2019 really began, just under ten years on from her death. The spring months had felt almost endless, a procession of lengthening days and overly intense blue skies. Life was fine. More than fine, it was good, perhaps the most comfortable it had ever been. That March I'd started work at a TV production company as a researcher, alongside my usual writing and journalism. It meant a good, stable income and the first opportunity I'd ever had to build some small savings and pay down some of my student debt, as well as freeing me up to commit myself to the kind of reporting I wanted to be doing. The work itself was good and it felt like I was good at it, too. The same month, I'd published my first report into the missing persons crisis, which took me aback with the force of its response. For days afterwards, I found myself replying to messages from people wanting to share their stories, or encouraging me to delve further into the shadows and the lives of those right on the cusp of sliding out of view. Some wanted to ask about practical help with locating their loved ones. Others, what I took as the chance to vent to someone they thought might be able to empathise.

It was just after midday on 21 May that year that I met Jacqueline Landy at her office for the first time, though we'd already spoken at length on the phone, a few months prior, just like I'd done with Joe Apps before our initial meeting in Vauxhall. Jacqueline has worked closely with death for almost her entire career, firstly as a funeral director and for the past eight years as the Cemetery and Crematorium Manager at West Norwood Cemetery, in south London. It's a perpetually demanding job for Lambeth Council, one of the city's largest local authorities, containing some of its most deprived wards. The grounds of West Norwood are themselves a historical curio, perhaps the least well known of London's 'Magnificent Seven' cemeteries, the self-consciously ornate solution to one of London's sporadic bursts of dangerous overcrowding in the nineteenth century. These days, its heavy gothic entrance sits at the end of an unprepossessing high street, a sharp reminder of a more wilfully ornate age. It didn't take long to find the right building, tucked a few yards inside the cemetery gates. Waiting at reception, I tried to think if I'd ever been in the grounds before, though nothing much came to mind outside of a couple of blurred reminders of making my way to the house of an old primary school friend, not too far away in Gipsy Hill. After a few minutes, Jacqueline appeared, with a smile and an unnecessary apology for keeping me waiting so long. In person, she gave off the same impression as she had on the phone; cheerful and precise, someone with the confidence of both experience and enjoyment in what she did for a living.

I was there to try and understand one of the parts of Jacqueline's job that seemed to me to speak to the idea of the returning missing just as much as Esther's story had. Only this concerned the dead, rather than the living. Every working day in West Norwood holds its own particular responsibilities. There are services to oversee and time-consuming admin to attend to. One crucial part of Jacqueline and her team's time is taken up with organising what are officially called public health funerals, for those who have died in Lambeth, in poverty, or without any next of kin to identify them and sometimes even without any clues to their identity at all. Public health funerals have been on the rise in Lambeth over the past decade, with 62 in 2010–11 up to 67 by the end of 2017–18,[24] the last year with a full record, just as they have been for ever more stretched councils all over the UK. As we settled down in her office, Jacqueline told me how it was tough to draw any set conclusions about the numbers in her patch, even if 'a rapid escalation is certainly something I've noticed though I [can't be certain] if that's due to austerity, or the cost of funerals, or whatever.' Of their total expenditure, just over half tends to go on funeral director costs, while each individual funeral costs between one and three thousand pounds, depending on factors like the religion of the deceased, the location of the funeral and whether it's a burial or cremation. These are not small details to Jacqueline and her team, but the very foundation of what they do. Their work runs on the proposition that every death deserves its own dignity, no matter its circumstances. A person has been found, their identity lost. The next step is to find out something, anything about the life they had led and prepare the most appropriate send-off.

Jaqueline's team have the authority to enter homes to try to find the clues that will hopefully give some shape to the story of the deceased. Anything will do – an address book, a picture, any snatched fragment of correspondence. It's all part of the process of identification. Sometimes it takes days, just as it might take weeks, until something comes up. Eventually, with luck, there might be someone to contact and tell the news of the passing. But it's not always so simple, even when someone relevant has been traced. They can be too estranged to care, or too poor – private funeral costs often run to many thousands of pounds. And there are those that cannot be found, including rising numbers of unknown immigrants, often young men, who have died in an alien land, too far from home to be remembered. When she spoke of them, I couldn't stop my thoughts drifting away to Christobal, even if Jacqueline was speaking primarily about people from further afield than Spain. If he ever felt that alone, in his worst moments. But how even then, he would have always had someone to vouch for his identity, no matter how bad things ever got here.

Jacqueline outlined the details of the process, even if no two searches are ever quite the same. 'We take whatever information we can get, even if it's just a name and hopefully a date of death. We could have nothing at all. We then start our own investigation, talking to neighbours and friends, who maybe have some details to offer,' she explained. 'But what normally happens is that we'd engage a genealogy company, based on the information we hold. If it's someone with a really common surname, James or Smith, then it could be that there are countless possibilities. But they'll pore through the electoral register and try to see if there's a wife or children to contact. It's very important to me that we let any relevant people know when and where the funeral is to take place. And when we have exhausted those options, we start to arrange it. It's a failsafe for us, in that we obviously don't want to cremate someone who did have a family. That has happened in the past, prior to genealogy.' The work isn't just a moral concern, but also a public health one. It doesn't always fit to be overly sentimental. Under Section 46 of the Public Health Act 1984 there is a clause that states if nobody comes forward, then the relevant local council must dispose of the body. 'If you could imagine a body in the mortuary that is – and it's not a nice image – decomposing, then you have to do something about it,' Jacqueline added matter-of-factly.

The council's service is a simple affair and usually takes place early in the morning. It's often the case that even families who have formally 'abandoned the body' would like to be present, which means that attendance can sometimes be higher than expected. 'We're quite flexible about it. People have the right to say goodbye,' Jacqueline said. If the search has thrown up any proof or compelling clues about the person's interests, they are often accounted for during the funeral itself. Once, the team discovered an Elvis CD in an elderly man's bedroom. At his cremation, they chose to play some of the most famous hits at the close of the service. About half an hour into our conversation, I wanted to know more about those that were 'found'. What about the families of loved ones that didn't abandon the body? It's true, Jacqueline responded, that there are many people who are grateful for their work. Sometimes people have memories of the person who has died, an estranged cousin or uncle, or whoever they were to them in life. And yes, there are the families that will take on the funeral, but it's a less and less frequent occurrence these days. Often, she reiterated, it's not a question of choice. Many people simply can't afford it. With a background working as a funeral director, Jacqueline told me she understood the pressures of the job. After all, they were a business too, often requiring costs to be paid up front. Funeral poverty is a term that has caught on in the UK over the past decade, as those costs have doubled since 2004, according to SunLife Insurance, one of the world's largest insurance providers. It's estimated that the average cremation now costs £4,271, with a burial coming in at £4,798.[25] With one-third of people in the UK having less than £600 in savings,[26] these are often not readily available sums of money to pay in the event of a bereavement. There are regional variations in the cost of death. The average London funeral runs to £5,963, almost £2,500 more than in Northern Ireland.[27] Of all the bills and stresses that make up a life, it isn't always the most pressing. Who wants to sit and think about the inevitable future loss of a loved one and the strain it might cost to give them the 'appropriate' send-off?

Over the last few years of her life, Gran spoiled me – there's no other word for it. She'd slip me a bit of extra pocket money almost every week, batting away my weak protestations with a smile and the reminder that 'there won't be anything left when I'm gone'. I'd spend it on clothes mostly, tracksuits and trainers that she'd beam at, even if she didn't quite understand why they needed to be quite so baggy or flamboyant. Her savings, everything that she left behind, would be enough to pay for her cremation at a Co-op funeral home, not a penny more or less. It still seems to me like a good way to do things, if you have the choice. In the end, her small savings meant we didn't need to worry about paying for her send-off, just as we didn't need to worry about Mum's the decade before.

How did we arrive at a point where dying in the UK costs more than anywhere else in Europe? One funeral director quoted in a piece in *Investment Week* described the trade's unique 'advantages'. Funerals, the anonymous insider said, 'are the ultimate distress purchase, made infrequently by inexpert, emotionally vulnerable clients'. To follow this brutal economic logic, rising costs aren't just something to be applauded as good for business, they're an inevitability. Grief-stricken people aren't so likely to be shopping around for a bargain – who wants to haggle in the face of a loved one dying – and will simply put up with whatever is presented to them. Of course, it doesn't always work that way. It isn't that people don't want to pay, but that they can't. The figures involved are so high that they can appear an abstraction. One in ten people in the UK do not have savings of any description, let alone for an unpredictable and often unforeseen cost like a funeral. People can pull themselves into trouble, trying to give a loved one a 'proper' goodbye, plunging into debt that can often feel shameful to carry around on their shoulders. No one wants to feel like they've failed their dead. It felt to me that not all that much had changed since the 1963 publication of *The American Way of Death*, Jessica Mitford's classic study of funeral practices in the US, either there or here. A world of slick, profit-run business and mandatory upselling, preying on people's most vulnerable, grief-stricken moments. But the last few years have seen something of a fightback, though progress is slow and painstaking, with charities like the London-based Quaker Social Action advocating for change and the widespread adoption of what should be a simple precept. That a decent goodbye shouldn't come with such crippling cost.

In 2017, the Scottish charity Community Renewal started work on Caledonia Cremation, the country's first non-profit funeral directors. A few years prior, the charity's CEO, Paul McColgan, had experienced a traumatic death in his own family. His brother-in-law had died suddenly in his 20s, without anything left behind to cover what had been an unforeseen, almost unfathomable event. Fortunately, there had been other family members who could step in and help cover costs. Funeral poverty had been pushing one in seven Scottish families into debt, he'd discovered. Something had to change. It wasn't right, that the cost of a death was financial punishment, as well the obvious strains of bereavement. The new enterprise launched in February 2018. Caledonia Cremation's offer is straightforward: a direct cremation for £995 for anyone anywhere in Scotland, wealthy or poor, from the Central Belt to the most remote island in the Outer Hebrides. Of course, it doesn't work for everyone. Some families will want something more extravagant, as is their right. Direct cremation doesn't come with a service or ceremony, with the body often taken straight from the mortuary or hospital. The family can choose to attend, but numbers are often limited, the process over before it's really begun. Still, there is a level of support and aftercare. An acknowledgement of what the family or loved ones are going through.

A couple of months after my first meeting with Jacqueline in West Norwood, I spoke to Angela Johnstone, bereavement adviser and funeral operative at Caledonia Cremations. She's been there from November 2017 and can't quite imagine herself doing anything else. Before we started, she'd warned that a client might ring at any time as she sat in the kitchen of her home in Glasgow, but we were free to speak until then. Work was busy, but then it was always busy. '[Our model] has really shaken up the whole industry in Scotland. You can't turn on the telly now without seeing an advert [for direct cremation]. There's a feeling that people can't get away with charging thousands and thousands for cremation services. You wouldn't believe the amount of people who don't know where to turn when someone dies. They don't have the money and haven't made any plans. It's a real issue for so many families,' Angela explained to me. The first call with any bereaved family usually comes within 24 hours after the death. 'You can hear how numb they are just in their voice. When I follow up the next day you can hear them getting a bit sharper, day by day. I'm always mindful about that first call. Only a tiny per cent of it is ever going in, the rest is just white noise.' Angela told me she's lucky to do the job she does. There's no way she could go to a profit-driven funeral directors now, not with what she's learned over the past three years. 'I worked in child protection before moving into a part-time minimum wage post in funerals because I wanted a totally different kind of career. Within a week, I knew I was never going to be able to do that upselling, going up to eight or nine thousands pounds.'

I thought about the collection of ashes that sit safely in my aunt's home in Derbyshire. That's where Mum and Gran sit now, the two of them reunited and returned to us. I'd been far too young to have anything to do with helping to organise either funeral and felt another surge of relief, both at that and the fact there had been enough money to cover them both without too much stress.

Months before, as I'd made my way home from meeting Jacqueline Landy that first time in West Norwood, I didn't feel much like being in the house. Instead, I decided to take myself to another familiar place to cure the restlessness I felt building in my head. My current home is just a few minutes' walk from the gates of Nunhead Cemetery, another of the 'Magnificent Seven' and only 15 minutes or so by foot from Honor Oak Crematorium. Like so many of London's burial grounds, Nunhead had suffered from several decades of neglect by the end of the twentieth century. At one time it was common enough for vandals to break in and defile the graves and ostentatious monuments to the Victorian worthies buried below. What the vandals couldn't achieve, nature did. The cemetery had been abandoned, too full and too expensive to devote much care to. As the years passed, the very fabric of the place changed. From lawn to meadow and, finally, to woodland. In the 1980s, a few dedicated locals formed the Friends of Nunhead Cemetery, to try and tame some of the wildness and protect the unloved ground. Today, it can often feel like a strange mixture of things. One part urban heritage site, another part makeshift nature reserve. In the summer, I can often hear the parakeets from my perch in the back garden, trilling their songs from the dense scrubs of greenery at the still wild and overgrown eastern fringes of the cemetery.

Most days, I find myself walking there. It doesn't really matter what time of year, there's always something to recommend it. When the sky is heavy and low, it can feel like a sinister place, an oppressive silence billowing out over things. The sort of mood that turns an afternoon stroll into a furtive affair. But spring transforms it, from gloom to something else, somewhere abundant and almost joyful. Most of the time, I make my way to the cemetery to avoid something in my day-to-day life. Some tedious chores or admin, or work I've found myself stuck with, on interminable Tuesday afternoons when my brain feels like sludge in my skull. Occasionally, I'll swing by some of the absurd monuments and crypts built to honour the wealth of this or that long-forgotten industrialist, but mostly I find my feet drawn to the edges of the overgrowth, where the years have half-rubbed off the names on the cracked gravestones jutting out the ground like broken teeth. It would take a strange person not to wonder at the identities they once represented. Or when the last person came to deposit flowers and stop a while, thinking of their loss. How they too had grown old and perhaps moved away, or stopped feeling the pull of duty to this particular place.

When I got home that same night after seeing Jacqueline, I couldn't stop thinking about what we'd spoken about. How her days are spent on the case of the people that have died missing and would stay that way for ever unless some clue is found that unlocks some of the secrets of the life they'd led. Something made me take to Facebook, a platform I'd barely used since 2017, aside from haunting the groups where the missing were being searched for. Scrolling through the ghostly newsfeed full of baby photos from half-forgotten schoolmates or urgent appeals for reliable south London plumbers, I still wasn't sure exactly what I was looking for.

There have been many times over the last decade that I'd typed variations of Christobal's name into the search bar, as I'd mentioned to Joe Apps back in Vauxhall. But something about that day made me think of something more specific about his memory. It must have been around 2001 or 2002, only a couple of years after the trip to La Línea not long after Mum's death. The long rambling letter that had arrived at 197C Honor Oak Road, written in his distinctive closely cropped handwriting. Most of its contents remain a blur, but there was a central message that has never faded. He was ok, he wrote, living in a monastery in northern Spain, an attempt to really get himself cleaned up and sorted out. Among the lines of apology and self-justification, there was a question. What were Lambeth Council giving me and was there any way that he qualified for payments too? It wasn't the letter of a well man, in body or mind. As I scrolled idly through search results of other Garcias from around the world, the thoughts of the day started to mature. What if that monastery was his final living quarters, far away from his Andalusian home? It felt comforting to know that he would not have died unmourned by his loved ones, like so many of Jacqueline's bodies, unless some powerful estrangement had occurred with his family in the years after I'd last seen him. It wasn't an outcome that seemed plausible somehow. They just didn't feel like that sort of clan, no matter how errant or troubled one of their members might be. Living or dead, I couldn't, or didn't want to, imagine him abandoned at his greatest moment of need. There was part of me that wanted to see this for myself, to see the city he'd called home again, if only just to make these thoughts seem more solid than they were in my mind alone. The idea of setting foot in La Línea again was slowly starting to occupy me in a way it hadn't since early childhood.

From May 2019, the months continued to blur. My reporting had started to take me in various competing directions and the occasional bouts of amateur sleuthing became slightly more focussed. As the summer rolled on, I kept in touch with Jacqueline. After that first meeting, I'd asked if it might be possible to attend one of their services, something she said wouldn't be a problem. The first few opportunities came and went. I'd be booked up or out of town, or some other circumstance would change at the very last minute. In late July, we'd had to reschedule after the family of one of the deceased had come forward and pledged to attend the funeral. Soon enough, the weather began to turn, from the heat and noise of the summer holiday months into something else, the onset of early autumn. The days grew shorter and the overcast skies more persistent and malicious.

Finally, we pencilled in a date. On 22 September there were to be two funerals, one at 8.30 a.m. and one at 9, a woman first, then a man, which Jacqueline said were ok for me to attend. On the day itself, I wondered what to wear, or what my role was. Who was I to the people that had passed? Not a mourner exactly, I supposed, but a witness. Was that right? Was that what I was to be that day? It didn't occur to me that there might be nerves, but that's precisely what I could feel in my stomach as I woke up not long after dawn to hear a thick, aggressive rain pounding against the table outside my bedroom window. Having selected a shirt and trousers, I tried to order a cab and felt the blood rushing to my head as order after order cancelled due to the conditions outside. I'd never attended a funeral in the rain, I thought stupidly as I finally clambered into the back of a car after the tenth attempt at booking. As we squeezed across the packed streets, my knuckles tightened. Late – that's all I could think – I was going to be late to the first service. It felt like the conclusion to a particularly charged anxiety dream, stuck in endless traffic on the fringes of Tulse Hill, late to a funeral of which you're supposed to be the only attendee. I plunged my hands into my jacket pockets and tried to breathe through the sharp sense of shame that had started to build. Eventually something cleared and the car pulled ahead, five minutes after the first service was already due to start. Jacqueline was understanding. 'Good old rain,' she responded to my panicked email just before the car pulled to a halt at the cemetery gates.

The water hammered down into the immaculately trimmed grass and snaked across the winding concrete path leading up to the crematorium. Suddenly everything felt small against the sky, as my field of vision started to shrink and blur. There was something else too, inside my stomach. The tight, almost rigid feeling that I remembered from the morning of Gran's funeral, a decade before. On the long approach to the building I tried to pick up my pace, to reach it before my clothes soaked through entirely. Gradually, I drew closer and realised how ridiculous I must have looked, a half-drowned visitor shuffling along the deserted path. But soon enough, I realised the previous service must have ended and that I was no longer alone. There was a woman just about visible in the middle distance, coming towards me from the crematorium, a small woman wrapped tight in a brightly coloured waterproof. As we passed, our eyes locked momentarily and I offered up a weak smile of acknowledgement, which she reciprocated. She must have been a mourner, there was no other explanation. Someone who had shown up after all to pay their respects. I tried to swallow my curiosity and the urge to call after her. Jacqueline had mentioned that there might be someone at the first service, which I'd forgotten in the chaos of the morning. It was none of my business to find out more. Who knows what that morning had cost her? Maybe she was an old friend, or even partner, someone who had known the dead woman in her best days and had only found out about her service at the last moment. Or she might just have been a neighbour or an old acquaintance, attending from a sense of it just being the right thing to do. Soon, her figure receded into the distance, lost against the mist. There was nothing else to feel but relief by the time I finally reached the crematorium itself, a squat brick building with an imposing oak front door. On arrival I shook hands with a tall thin man with large mournful eyes from Jacqueline's team who was to serve as the officiator for the non-religious service. After a few words of small talk and the chance to wipe the rain from my eyes, it was time to begin. Having taken a seat at the very back of the room, all there was to do was await my instructions, as bashfully as a child might.

Just a few feet away there was a man lying there who had lived a life that neither I, nor the officiator, knew the first thing about. His life was not something available to make sense of. In death, he had become one of the missing. And now he was found, even if the other mysteries remained and would remain. As we moved through the service I tried to keep my eyes pinned to the floor, out of what I hoped was respect. But it was something more than just respect alone. There was fear too in the knowledge of what was about to come. The moment when the coffin would move down into the inevitable, into the fires that would turn the man's body into dust. As the officiator spoke at the pulpit, I tried to strain my ears to the shape of his words, but I could feel my mind somewhere else. No, it wasn't back to the summer of 2009, in the oak-panelled room where we had said goodbye to Gran. It felt further away, all the way to Mum's cremation in 1999. The queasy realisation of not knowing where to look, of not quite knowing what it is that is being expected of you. The feeling soon passed. I was here to bear witness to this man's life, as the only mourner in a building designed to hold many people's grief. This was not about the tangles of my past. This was about being here, now. I looked up and began to follow along, standing when it was required and keeping my eyes fixed on the coffin, my ears trained on the words about loss and forbearance. In the brief pauses between the words hit the sound of rain, still falling hard outside on the earth and concrete.

After the service ended, I spoke briefly to the two members of Jacqueline's team who stood at the door, while trying to suppress the odd, almost queasy feeling in my stomach. For them, this was another day's work. They had seen this before; it wasn't something strange or new to them as it was for me. They were kind and asked if I had any questions, but I couldn't quite find my tongue or anything that felt right to say or ask. Instead, I offered another stiff handshake and made my way down to the office to say goodbye to Jacqueline and return to the high street and the number 68 bus that would take me into central London. After the quiet of the morning, the bus felt deafening as the sound of competing phone calls mingled with the hum of the engine and the rattle of thoughts in my own head. The rain had made the windows cloud over and I soon lost track of what suburban arterial road we were moving down. People got up and others replaced them. As we passed Camberwell, the bus filled up with primary school children on their way to an outing, their laughter and noise filling up the entire top deck. Their teacher looked tired, you could tell by the way she sat down, all at once with a slightly glazed look in her eyes. It seemed obvious which adults were which, the teacher and the supporting volunteer parents, some who looked almost as giddy as the children.

Watching the life around me made the events of the morning already feel like something very far away. I'd been on a few day trips like that in my own past, many years ago. One memorable one had been to the Natural History Museum in South Kensington, a place of almost ecstatic joy for so many generations of small children. I suppose I must have been about six, at the height of my comically intense dinosaur phase, an obsession which consumed all of my energies and I imagine those of the adults in my life. There's no way of forgetting the excitement of that morning, the thrilling sense of adventure and the wonders that the day was promised to hold.

The coach left Fairlawn Primary early with me and Christobal sitting together, wrapped up in a state of mutual exhilaration. Who, you might have wondered, was more thrilled, father or son? His face had broadened into a grin almost the second we'd left the flat. The memories of the day still carry something of the epic sense of anticipation. Staring out of the window at all the grand and unfamiliar parts of the city. Soaking in the main events of the collection and staring up at the vast reconstructions of bloodthirsty carnivorous and their pliant herbivore cousins. The gift shop and the lurid keyring that Christobal had bought me, showing what I took to be a velociraptor staring out from the plastic with murderous intent. And later, how we returned home to regale Mum with the full day's action, in all of its almost overwhelming glory. How could it ever be possible to forget one of those moments when things really seem to make sense, however fleetingly. The magic of one ideal day, where the rest of our lives contradictions held tight, or were even forgotten. Back in the present, the bus drifted down Walworth Road and as I looked across at the children talking excitedly on the top deck, something else started to shift. To the morning that had just gone and the man whose funeral I had just attended, who had passed without another witness to the life that he had led. I thought about the fire that had raged beyond the sight of his coffin and memories of other fires that had consumed the bodies of people that I've loved. And if Christobal was no longer here, could a similar anonymous send-off have been his fate? The rain was starting up again, smearing the window and battering down against the concrete outside. Please God, I thought as the packed bus stood in the post-rush-hour traffic. Please don't let me die alone.

PART V
THE LEFT-BEHIND

CHAPTER 11

It was the end of my second day in Glasgow and the sky had long since set to dark as the first few office workers started to dribble out of their buildings and into another Tuesday evening in the depths of midwinter in 2020. The day had been clear, a February rarity in the city, which meant the cold felt that bit harsher as I checked my way across the city centre to Queen's Street station, walking with a quickening flow of relieved rush-hour commuters heading back into the temporary respite of the suburbs. I was early for the 6.01 train to Edinburgh, but not to the point of discomfort. There was plenty of time for a cup of tea and a chance to stand back alone and observe the mismatch of bodies rushing through the station's half-refurbished shell. Maybe it was just nostalgia or something else, but I couldn't help remembering how much smaller the old station felt around the time I first got to know Jamie Reid, the old friend I was on my way to meet for a long overdue catch-up.

It's odd enough to remember, but for a while back then I suppose Queen Street was something like a second home. In the summer of 2012 I was still living an hour and a half north east of Glasgow in Dundee, three-quarters of the way through the undergraduate degree in English that had accelerated rapidly from boredom to perhaps too much fun in the blink of an eye. It was a short era, and a good one. Friendships had solidified and work had intensified without too much stress, as the city had started to feel, if not like home, then at least a comfortable enough place to exist in for the time being. Life ran along predictable lines, not quite adolescence, not yet adulthood. It was a time when work meant providing for the twin necessities of rent and 'going out', with anything else usually a luxury beyond contemplation. I suppose I thought that I knew it all. That this was all happening for the very first time. That I was the first to worry about deadlines and campus gossip, or experiment with substances and creative methods of everyday self-sabotage. The weeks took their dignity serving a supporting role as the long approach to the weekend, the focal point of all our lives. Thursday, Friday, Saturday. They were the frontispiece and main event. If it wasn't Dundee, it was Glasgow – on a train boarded straight after the close of one of my shifts at Marks & Spencer, after a long day stocking the rails on the schoolwear section and trying what I imagined was my best not to lose it with the most entitled of the middle-aged Saturday shoppers. From Dundee to Queen's Street and back, twice a week, an hour and a half each way – just enough time to analyse whatever triumphs and embarrassments had occurred the night before.

Things changed again with the new year, in 2013. It wasn't that things got heavier in Dundee exactly, but they weren't the same. Suddenly, it was clear that adulthood wasn't just a state of charmed weightlessness, wasn't just a procession of blurred weekends and drifted weeks. I didn't understand it like this, then. But there were casualties to even our tame hedonism, of the sort that couldn't have been ignored, even if we had wanted to. There was Karl who had to retreat home to his parents after his behaviour had become unignorable and erratic. The signs had been there, but who had really wanted to face them? He was part of a wider friendship group, closer to others than to me, but things were tighter then, at the point where it still feels normal to spend most of your time in company, often doing not very much at all. He was usually there, tucked somewhere on the margins of vision, rolling endless cigarettes to keep his hands busy, as we loitered in the bedroom of whoever's house share we happened to find ourselves in. You would notice how his wrists shook slightly, whenever he took a break from crafting the tobacco into his stash of razor thin silver papers. As the weekends went past, his presence stopped being taken for granted. He'd always enjoyed his solitude, but hours had become days, would have become weeks if he hadn't been forced to leave for seminars, or prompted by our concerns. Something was messing with Karl's head, everyone agreed. And by the spring, that was it. I never quite established whether he had volunteered to leave or whether his family had instigated it,

not that it really mattered. Of course, it was the right thing
– no one questioned that. But the months slipped by and his
absence ceased to be remarked upon by anyone outside of
our friendship group. There were messages exchanged, we
knew he was safe enough back home and was as 'alright' as
could be expected or understood inside our narrow vocab-
ularies.

It was in February 2013 that I first met Jamie Reid, in
the smoking area of a nightclub in Dundee. Though things
had almost begun to have consequences, you couldn't help
feeling lighter in his company. He always had a way to
make things feel a bit easier somehow. Often, his approach
would be heard, rather than seen – just as it still is all these
years later. Subtlety was never really his chief talent. You'd
be standing in a smoking area and hear the boom of his
voice, just before feeling the clasp of his arm on your
shoulder. It was always like that: dull nights would gather
energy, good nights would accelerate into something more
memorable. Jamie always had that gift, impossible to name
or ignore. He just made people feel like themselves. Unlike
most of my immediate friendship group in Dundee, he
wasn't a student, but worked as a window cleaner for a
local business that sent him around the city at all kinds of
unsociable hours. More times than I really care to mention,
we'd knock into one another in the dawn hours. Me, stumbling home from excess; him, on his way to work in the
city centre, with a cheerful laugh or two at my expense.
'Fuck's sake, Cisco,' I can still remember him cackling with

a shake of the head, as I'd throw him a slightly dazed wave.

In that time, in that place, it really did feel like we were living in a tight-knit community, with Jamie just one part of a dense little universe. There were classes and club nights, pub trips and long, aimless days spent in various student flats dotted around the city centre and the west end of Dundee. Often, it felt as safe as the womb. When reality did occasionally find its way in, as with Karl's troubles, it could still feel like an aberration. We had hundreds of friends and acquaintances from all over the world, packed tightly into a Scottish coastal city of under 150,000 people. The outside world existed, but mostly with the recognition that it was for a later date. All that really mattered in those last two years in Dundee was life as we were leading it. And then, in the summer 2014, it was over. Graduation and the subsequent dispersal. Some went to London, others to Glasgow and Edinburgh. Others even went abroad to Europe, or further afield. I decided to take my chances in Glasgow on a hastily set-upon MA, to share a dismal ground-floor flat with my closest friend from Dundee. Karl, as far as I knew, was still living with his parents. It is still to my shame that I can't vouch for his whereabouts any further than that.

Not everyone left Dundee that summer. Jamie was still there, for one. Where else could he have been, at that time? For him, the city wasn't just a place to temporarily alight on and then leave after picking up a degree. It had always been home, or at least near enough, having grown up a few miles over the Tay Bridge in Newport, one of a cluster of small towns that sit directly opposite Dundee itself. The year 2014 was also a landmark in 21-year-old Jamie's life, though nothing like the gentle epoch change the rest of us had celebrated.

On Wednesday, 22 January, Jamie's mum had been reported missing. The appeal published in the *Dundee Courier* three days later sketched the basic details. Susan Reid, 56, 5 feet 7 inches, slim with blonde/greying hair, a part-time librarian at the University of Dundee, where she had failed to report for work that week. Jamie had been quoted in the piece, telling the paper just how unlike his mum it was, how obviously beside themselves he and their loved ones were. 'My mum has never done anything like this before so that's the most worrying thing,' he told the local reporter. 'She would usually get in touch with me if she was going to be going away for even a little bit of time.' They had exchanged texts on the Tuesday, as the day passed normally enough. On the Wednesday, Jamie texted again, this time to no reply. Something was wrong. The police were called, a report quickly written up and circulated. The rest of the week passed without any news or reliable sightings. Soon, lifeboat crews from nearby Broughty Ferry were out searching the river for any sign of her, without success. That weekend, Susan's local church held a prayer vigil for her safe return, while her sister and mother travelled down the coast from Aberdeen to help with the hunt. One of the biggest strains came with deciding what to tell Jamie's father, who lived with advanced multiple sclerosis in the family home in Newport. His long-term memory was still ok, though he often struggled with anything short term. Susan was a full-time carer, as well as a mother and wife. It was decided that he wouldn't be told about her vanishing, not yet anyway. There would only be confusion and pain to come from it, if they did.

The passing months were only to bring their fair share of both. Where could she have gone? And how could you stop your thoughts from running to the worst? Though Susan hadn't gone missing before, she shared a common denominator with eight in ten missing adults in the UK: a history of mental illness. For years, she had lived with anxiety and depression, to the point of being signed off work at the university library in the past. Weeks went by. It seemed impossible, but life found its inevitable way of carrying on, in its own way. Support came from the local community, friends stepped up and rallied round. There were a few markers of normality to be clung on to, club nights to be attended, pub trips to be undertaken. But none of it was anything like normal. The police were stumped, after those first few dramatic weeks, even after the search had widened and intensified. They had offered a few competing theories, some of which had seemed to Jamie to be both insensitive and far-fetched. Perhaps she had been having an affair, and had run away to be with him, this mystery apparition? It would have been almost laughable, if the stakes hadn't been so high. One month, turned to two, turned to three, with no end to the dread and uncertainty that had shaded everything from the day of her disappearance.

The state of limbo lasted until 25 March 2014, when Susan Reid's body was found by a man walking his dog in Tentsmuir Forest, only a few miles from her home. There's a piece in the *Evening Telegraph*, another of Dundee's local papers, published just a few days after, publicly confirming the terrible news with a few more quotes from Jamie. Of course, the previous months had been a private hell, 'but now we can give her a proper send-off and a proper memorial service. It's been the hardest few months of my life, but it's definitely given me some closure and I can try to move on.' One of the most difficult things, he continued, would be explaining it to his father, who still didn't know what had happened and had been moved to a care home paid for by Fife Council, after Susan's disappearance. It was a huge loss, not just to the family, but to the whole community around Newport. She had been part of so many people's lives. The funeral was still to be arranged, which was set to be a 'really good celebration of her life', as Jamie put it himself. And almost exactly one year later, to the day, in March 2015, Jamie's father passed away at the care home in Fife. Jamie had been together with him at the last.

On the train into Edinburgh Waverley, I tried to remember the last time I'd properly seen Jamie, outside of perhaps a snatched pint on one of my periodic visits up to Scotland for work. Surely, it couldn't have been before I'd moved back to London in 2015. But why not? Time has its ways of wreaking havoc with perspective. There was no reason why this should be any different. It's one of the clichés you can't avoid, the truism you'd hear from the adults all your life: time speeds up with age. It's alarming, how quickly they were being proved right. One minute you're 20, broke and terminally bored, sitting in the middle of a seemingly endless summer holiday in a deserted Dundee; the next, you find you're now the sort of person who stares out the window of a commuter train, sighing about a time that can't be lived through again.

After about an hour, the soft, pre-programmed voice of the automated conductor rang out to give warning of the final approach to the station. The previous week, Jamie and I had solidified our plan via Instagram direct messages. We needed a pub where we could talk properly, close enough to the station for the last train back to Glasgow for me, and somewhere easy enough for him to walk home from. Cafe Royal seemed like the best shout, a cheerfully ornate spot just a few minutes' walk away from Waverley. I saw Jamie almost as soon as I stepped off the platform, loitering at the agreed exit, looking as well as I'd ever seen him. We fell to talking almost instantly on our way to the pub, straight to stories of some of the old faces and a few of their current dramas. Instead of Glasgow drizzle, there was the bite of an east coast frost on the air, the start of a fine, clear night. As we smoked at the pub's entrance, more than anything else, I just tried to take in a bit of how good it felt to see an old friend.

Edinburgh has been Jamie's home since July 2017 when he and his then girlfriend – now wife – Heather moved down for a change of scenery in the middle of his social work studies at the University of Edinburgh. It seemed like a natural progression, after the worst days of 2014. The move felt like a dark cloud lifting from their shoulders. Back when things had been at their height, he had thrown some of his energy into raising money for the Scottish Association for Mental Health. It just seemed like the natural thing to do. The big fundraiser took place just two days after Susan's body had been found, in the form of a club night at the Reading Rooms, the now shuttered Dundee nightclub that served as a crucial pillar of support for Jamie. Increasingly, it seemed that he needed to get out and pursue something informed by the freshness of his own experiences. Something that would make him feel like he was using his energies for good. Social work had long appealed, even if Dundee still felt too close to home, so Jamie ended up applying to Edinburgh, who accepted him with an unconditional offer. After four years of study, he landed a job with Edinburgh Council, working with children with learning disabilities and their families, while Heather works in children's services.

The pub was bustling for a Tuesday, with suited office workers and noisy tourists jostling for attention at the bar. After settling down to a quiet table tucked in from the entrance, we started almost straight into the main topic of conversation. What, I wanted to know from someone else, it means to try and pick up the pieces after a loved one has disappeared of their own volition. 'The thing with my mum,' Jamie told me, 'is that we did find her. But there will always be that question of why, and the reminder of that feeling of having absolutely no idea where she might have gone. That was just for a few months. I don't know how people live with that for even longer and I don't want to imagine what that must feel like.'

Over our first drink I wondered if there is anything he would say now to his younger self, struggling through those long months of pain and uncertainty. 'I don't know,' he replied after a few seconds of deliberation. 'The thing is, I was lucky that I had good support around me. There were a lot of times when I was very low, before and after we found out that she had passed away. I was in a pretty vulnerable position to be honest. It might sound cheesy as fuck, but I would say that there is light at the end of the tunnel. If I could go back and tell my old self one thing, it would be that there will be positives to come out of this.'

It's an insight that only comes with the passing of the years. Perhaps it's something that everyone left behind must feel, at some point or another; one of the lesser realised stages of grief to go with the anger and guilt. After all, it isn't just death itself that takes courage in facing down and coming to terms with. It's also the knowledge that your life has come to be irrevocably altered by a chain of decisions or inevitable occurrences that you had no say in whatsoever.

It took a long time to understand this myself. How Mum's passing and Christobal's absence represented two different sides of the same loss and set the grooves of what was to come, both good and ill, almost entirely outside of anything I could have done to change things as a child. Jamie told me that he considers himself almost lucky in one sense and I think I know what he meant. '[Everything with my mum] sent me in a better direction than the one I'd been going down. My attitude has always been, "Right, well, no time to wallow, let's do something." My mum had always wanted me to go to uni. She'd get pissed off at me for fucking up at school and that. I've had the chance to go and do social work and try to give something back. That's one of the key factors about being a social worker. Empathy. If I've had the experiences that I've had, then maybe I can somehow use them to try and understand what someone else is going through. I didn't understand that overnight.'

It's funny, he explained over a fresh drink, to remember what life was like before January 2014. 'I was stuck [in my] fairly dead-end job cleaning windows, when everything happened. Whatever else it was, it was also a kick up the arse. My life was pretty comfortable, with my flat in Dundee, living with Heather, having fun at the weekends. But there wasn't any scope in that to progress. After Mum went missing, it made me think that the risk of moving to Edinburgh and starting my studies wasn't really a risk at all. What's the worst thing that could happen when the worst thing has already happened?'

I told him that I was certain that I knew what he meant this time. What's the risk of a new start put against the pain of losing your loved ones? And who can ever know, I said to myself just as much as to Jamie, what life would have looked like if none of it had happened at all. When I was younger, I'd occasionally let myself get lost in thought imagining what seemed to me the most gloriously banal counterfactuals of a life other than my own, that could have been true if Mum hadn't died, or Christobal had been a different person. Where we might have lived, or what Mum might have done for a living. If I would have learned to speak Spanish as a matter of domestic routine, or developed the same kinds of closeness I now try not to take for granted with my aunties and other close relatives. It felt like a novelty to say all of this aloud, to someone that I knew had an understanding of what it meant. But this was about Jamie, not my patchwork of recollections, I thought as I stopped for breath.

It was Jamie's turn to tell me he understood. Even at the start, it could feel like other people didn't really get how to approach him or the situation, outside of his core community of friends and loved ones. His work could have dealt with it better, he still thinks. '[Luckily] I was really friendly with my supervisor, who immediately said I could take a week off. After that went by, I said that there was no way I was going to be able to come back in, with everything that was going on. His bosses turned around and said they wouldn't supply compassionate leave. They wanted me to save the three days they'd offer me for a funeral, if and when there was one. I went back for a wee while, but my mate's dad was opening up a takeaway in St Andrews and offered me a job. I took it because they knew me well and I knew they understood. When Mum was eventually found, they gave me consistent paid time off and I'd only been there for a few weeks, really.'

It's not true, the idea that memories inevitably fade into the past. Some things are too vivid, too formative and raw. Some things stay present, no matter how much time passes and makes the past start to feel like something strange. The idea of one day erasing the worst days, or waking up to a magically definitive closure, is a fantasy, and not always a charmed one. It's something I've long known. And it's something Jamie knows himself, only too well. There can still be hard times. '[Although] people are a lot more understanding in social work about that sort of stuff,' he told me. 'The first thing I did when I got my job was tell my manager, look this is my background, this is why I wanted to do this. There have been times when I haven't been dealing with it well, and they understand that. If you treat your staff well then you'll get better work out of them, if you want to even look at it from that level.'

Jamie's life is mostly in Edinburgh now, but it probably won't be for ever. Though both he and Heather enjoy their jobs and the city, it remains one of the UK's most expensive places to live. When it comes to the next stage, of settling down into home ownership and other markers of sober-minded adulthood, the logical step seems like returning to Tayside. Specifically, Dundee.

Though certainly not Newport, the small town that carries the full burden of the past. 'The main reason I don't want to move back there is the obvious associations. That horrible feeling of, "Who am I going to run into that was my mum's pal?" It's those constant reminders of her not being here,' he explained. 'The house itself is bad because of the link to the missing episode itself. With Newport generally, it's more that she's passed away. People are obviously happy to see me and are happy for what I've achieved, but it can be exhausting sometimes too. It's the reminder of a previous life, when everything was different. It's a small town. At least from Edinburgh to Dundee, you're still in a city.'

Over the last few years, a new family ritual started up, though it's one that's already started to feel like it might have outlived its usefulness. In late January, Jamie, Heather and his mum's sister would walk from the old family home in Newport, tracing the miles on the route that Susan most likely took, from the house to the spot in the woods where she was found. In 2019, Jamie knew it would be the last time they did so. 'We'd do it on the anniversary. I know it sounds a bit morbid. We did it last year and I thought, "No, this is enough." I'd be fine on the day, but then it sparked this feeling of absolute dread, like that cloud of darkness again. The reality is that it's still really hard to deal with. It's [a feeling] I still get when I go back. There are all the

reminders of these little things that you might never actually think about normally.' It was just a few minutes later
that I decided to switch off the voice recorder and order us
another pint. The night was fairly young and I thought I
could sense we'd talked about the traumas of the past for
quite long enough.

What Jamie told me about his sensitivity to place and the
complexities of memory struck at something deep. I've long
had my own complicated relationship with home, or rather
just the place where it all happened to happen, all those
years ago. Forest Hill and its immediate surroundings can
feel like a trap, as well as a comfort. For every treasured
memory of an age long smoothed into history, there is
another thought, another recollection of something heavier
and long suppressed. When I first moved back in those
summer months of 2015, I knew I'd probably made a
mistake. The attic flat I was living in happened to overlook
the garden of the basement flat that had once signified a
new start for me and Mum, back in the mid-1990s. And in
fleeting moments, late at night when the light started to
creep unevenly across the walls, it really did feel like the
years had collapsed in on themselves and I was almost back
there, this time as an observer, not a participant, in the story
of my own life. That particular return only lasted ten
months, before I moved a couple of miles down the road to
my friend's mum's house in Nunhead. Short lived or not, it
was enough to start to know something about the ghosts of
the past, both friendly and unwelcome. It's still odd, to feel

my feet trace the same concrete that Christobal's would have as he stormed back into the night, on the way to God knows what excess. I wonder if he felt the same way I do about a place with such an unreal quality: half unremarkable suburb, half leafy fortress perched at the precipice of south-east London. Or if he perhaps never really noticed at all.

It might be an unforgivable superstition, but I've long believed that places soak up something of our moods, our anxieties and fears, serving to exacerbate them and make them feel somehow more real than they ever do in our minds alone. It's the feeling that some places just seem to hold on to their tragedies more deeply than others. Jamie told me how he wasn't the only person living in the shadow of the missing in Newport. 'There were some guys that I went to school with, their dad went missing. This was years ago now. He drove on to the Tay Bridge, where they found his car, but his body was never recovered. They don't know what happened. That we come from the same small town, that seems strange to me. I'm from Newport, they're from Wormit, just along the road. There seems to be a lot of tragedy from that area.'

It had just gone 11 when I realised my careful plan to catch the last train back to Glasgow was in with a serious chance of unravelling. Our conversation had moved on again, beyond both of our lost and missing people and back to gossip and tall tales from classic nights in the Dundee of 2013. Suddenly, the clock on my phone told me I was cutting it fine. We had time for a final smoke and Jamie walked with me down to the Princes Street entrance to Waverley station. And that was that, as he made his way back home for an earlyish night in preparation for work the next morning. I ended up making the train with five minutes or so to spare, settling into an almost deserted carriage and my thoughts of the night that had just passed. I was tired, in the way that comes after a bout of serious talk. It really felt like I'd only been watching the night through the window for a few minutes as the train pulled back into Glasgow Queen Street.

The older I get, the harder it is to keep track on all the different eras and epochs of my life. What are you supposed to do with them? When did one end and another begin? Is it possible to discern a thread running through them all, to make sense of all the randomness? Jamie was a friend who spanned a couple of them, from the old days in Dundee to whatever it was we were both living in now. I had to laugh at the idea of us meeting as the very epitome of respectable young professional men. It hadn't quite been like that, all those years before. After leaving the station, the city-centre streets were as wide and as empty as I'd ever seen them, as I walked back to the frigid comfort of my Airbnb in Finnieston, where I was staying alone. On arrival, I'd waited for the kettle to boil and looked across the tenement court-yard from my bedroom window, lazily thinking about all the different kinds of people sleeping behind the rows of closed blinds and curtains. Those who would be lying peacefully and the others who would be awake until the early hours, their eyes locked restlessly to the ceiling. From my vantage point I could see one other illuminated window, its light soft and comforting. I fancied I could make out a silhouette, though there was no way of telling whether it was that of a man or woman. For a few moments I kept my sight focussed on that little island in the darkness, before finishing my tea and switching off the bedside lamp. As I drifted off, it felt like thoughts of the old days were merging with the present and the future. Christobal was in Dundee, Jamie in London. And there I was, lying confused in a strange bed in a familiar city. But soon, none of that seemed to matter anymore as I fell into the deep sleep of exhaustion.

CHAPTER 12

There have been times over the past four years when Chloe Bornstein has had to take a step back from the search for her brother. In the spring of 2019, Chloe and I had exchanged several lengthy emails about her predicament. It seemed the easiest means of communication, with me in London, Chloe at her home in Colorado and a seven-hour time difference sitting between us. At 3.20 p.m. on the afternoon of 1 November 2016, her brother Peter Edwards had disembarked from the Stagecoach X7 bus that had taken him from Aberdeen to Stonehaven, an unremarkable seaside town on the north-east coast of Scotland. To his family, it seemed like he simply evaporated into thin air. The 65-year-old had served as a pastor a hundred or so miles to the south in Perthshire, where he lived and had helped found Perth Christian Fellowship Church in the 1980s. Peter was a popular man, well known and liked in the local community. The subsequent police report after his disappearance fleshed out the slim figure on the granular CCTV footage. Peter Edwards, 65 years old, 5 feet 9 inches, balding, with a full grey beard, sideburns and gold-rimmed glasses. His clothes were just as understated. A long-sleeved grey shirt, black tank-top jumper, tie, grey trousers and black leather shoes. Peter still spoke with an American accent, despite all of his years in Scotland. The next few days witnessed the usual things: door-to-door enquiries, a review of the bus's surveillance footage, the public appeal for anyone with any information to call Police Scotland on 101.

In January 2017, it was reported in the local Perthshire press that the search had gone cold. Nothing in the case seemed to make any sense. It seemed entirely out of keeping with Peter's life. There were few clues or traces of a motive. No sudden fracture that had occurred that might have explained away his disappearance. In the years since, there has been no news of his whereabouts, aside from an occasional trickle of renewed media interest, usually instigated by Chloe, many hundreds of miles away from her home in the US. The distance has hardly made the situation any easier. Peter's wife in Scotland believes that he is dead, Chloe wrote to me. A deeply religious woman, she is certain because Jesus came to her in a dream with news of her husband's passing. But Chloe still isn't sure; how could she be, with no other shred of proof aside from divine intervention? She told me that she can feel the opposite pull, that her brother is still out there somewhere. That his disappearance was a calculated act, the first step in a new life far away from the cares of the old. This is the basic story. But there is more, Chloe told me. She is sure Peter planned everything in advance even if all she is now left with are questions. One theory is that he had met someone in Stonehaven immediately upon his arrival who quickly spirited him away. 'No body washed up to shore. No body [has been] found. He is out there. I would feel it if he had passed. The sniffer dogs did not pick up his scent in Stonehaven. He was not spotted on any CCTV footage anywhere in the town. No one saw him there. Not a trace of him. This could only be if he [had] never [actually been] there. We believe a vehicle waited for him there at the bus stop.' There were many things that Chloe asked me to leave out of what I wrote. There was much more to be said, though it would have to wait, she wanted me to understand. At the time of writing, Chloe hadn't given up on seeing Peter again. There was still hope. Until whatever resolution might be to come, she had to keep hope. Her brother's vanishing had opened up a rupture in her life and the lives of her extended family. There were the facts and whatever speculation felt appropriate. And there was the constant pain of not knowing. I wanted to write to Chloe to tell her that I understood, that I knew, that we shared some intimate knowledge of what it meant to be marked by the missing. But that wasn't quite right; there wasn't a direct equivalence. Her pain was raw. My thoughts of Christobal were complicated, but they didn't carry the same fresh, relentless intensity.

Just like the missing, the left-behind are an eclectic constituency, their diversity a powerful reminder of how many lives can be touched by the fact of a single missing person. Some, like Jamie, have lived through the long days of painful ambiguity and worry, to arrive at the knowledge of what happened to their loved one. If not closure, it is something. Life can move past the endless feedback loop of speculation and uncertainty. Then there are those like Chloe, still searching, still holding on to hunches and clues as to what might have happened. Things aren't always quite so neat.

Our exchange felt a long time in the past by the first week of May 2020, when I received an email from Danny Crewe. It was around six weeks into lockdown and things were starting to take on a slightly surreal quality, as the outside world shrank down to the purely local, to be measured by the same two or three easy walks from my home. My February trip to Scotland and my meetings with Jamie and Hester Parr were the last time I had left the confines of south-east London, yet alone the city itself, months before I'd made it to Dundee or Newcastle. The idea of a contemplative late-night train journey between Glasgow and Edinburgh already felt like an impossibly glamorous relic of a decadent, long-gone age. It was just after 5 p.m. when the message arrived in my Gmail account, with the subject line 'Missing persons advice?' It wasn't the first time I'd received something similar, though none had been quite so detailed. Danny had read about my work on the book on Twitter and had a few questions about people who were difficult to locate, specifically his missing father. Our stories weren't all that dissimilar, although Danny had no concrete memories at all of a man that had left before he was born, only to return for a couple of years before he vanished again, this time for good. It was a practical email, as its heading suggested. His dad had been a heroin addict, living as chaotically as that implied. No, he didn't tend to lose any sleep about his absence, but that didn't mean he wasn't looking for answers, for his own sake if nothing else. He was curious, just to know something of the man's existence other than the scraps he'd gleaned from his mum and various family friends over the years. At 26, he reckoned he was as ready as he was ever going to be to find out what had happened to a man he'd never really known. The Salvation Army family-tracing service hadn't thrown up any useful leads, but that had been a while ago now and he was ready to try again. Was there anywhere or anyone I could recommend who might be able to help, and how was my own journey going towards finding out some answers about my past?

Amidst the strangeness of the pandemic, the message came as a jolt, though not an unwelcome one. Work hadn't stopped, but my usual methods had been forced to change. Instead of the face-to-face meetings I was used to, reporting boiled down to the limits of the phone and video call. Danny's message instantly made me take stock. Where was I really, in myself and my thoughts of Christobal? There wasn't an obvious answer, in truth. Everything had been reduced to the strange and small, with much of the world ushered indoors in the face of a novel horror.

If the idea of central London or Scotland felt surreal, then Andalusia was entirely unknowable, a speck beyond my mental horizon, even if there was now plenty of free time to chew over the tangles of the past in my mind. In reply to Danny, I tried to answer his questions, recommending Missing People as a potential avenue for help with tracking his father, thinking of how kind and thorough Kirsty Hillman had been when she had explained how their tracing system Lost Contact worked. Aside from that I wanted to know if he might be interested in talking to me in more depth. It wasn't all that often someone got in touch with a story at least so superficially similar to my own and I thought that it might be interesting, hopefully even useful, for both of us. There was something in his tone that had felt familiar. Something precise and studiedly matter of fact that I recognised in the image that I'd long presented to myself and others. It wasn't false in any conscious way. I still believed in the mantra of this being the right time to delve into my past, how I was an adult capable of logical, dispassionate curiosity, even regarding something so elemental and deep rooted. The same thing was present in Danny's words, with their carefully judged seriousness. About a week passed between my reply and his response to my request. It was no problem, he wrote. In fact, he'd be happy to talk.

It had just gone 7 p.m. in early June when I picked up the phone and called Danny's mobile. His accent seemed familiar, flecked with suburban north London from his upbringing in Enfield. Just now, he was studying for an MA up north at Lancaster University. There were worse places to be. At least he had his car and easy enough access to local beauty spots in the Lake District. 'It wasn't quite the same lockdown I'd be having in London,' he added with a laugh. After ten minutes of polite preamble, we started on the missing. 'Two and two came together when I saw something about the book, that [we shared] similar situations, in terms of a father figure being absent. I was thinking about sending an email for a while.' Danny started to flesh out the story he'd told in his first message. His parents had met in the early 1990s, while his mum was at Middlesex University studying international development. The two hit it off quickly after meeting at a house party they'd both arrived at by chance. Their connection was immediate. 'They met up over the summer and she was pregnant not that long after. He had been straight up when he heard the news and told her that he had quite serious substance abuse problems. After that, he made the call to leave that first time and came back after two and a half years. He was back again briefly and then left again [and] that was it.' There's a retro, almost quaint detail that Danny has found to particularly stick in his mind from that period, even if he was far too young to remember it himself. As his mum tells it, she would stick posters around local newsagents and other shops in the area after his dad's first disappearance. Handmade offerings bearing his name and the plea to please get in touch with any information, with a landline number posted at the bottom of the page. 'That somehow worked,' Danny added slightly disbelievingly. 'He was probably still in Enfield. He was back in the picture for a bit after that. He must have still been using. [It's] like the people that keep coming back and going again, the root cause hadn't been addressed. And then he left for good, not long afterwards.'

Danny mentioned luck early on in our conversation. He was raised by his mum, who he has always been close to, which is something he has never taken remotely for granted. She has never kept anything back about what she knows and remembers about his dad, something Danny is also thankful for. But so much time has passed now, smoothing memories into something almost unreal for her as well as him. And what does he really know, aside from his dad's addiction and vanishing? His dad's family had lived in Islington, though he grew up near Torbay in Devon, on the south-west coast of England. He'd enjoyed his football and stood at a fairly average height. He'd had a brother, Danny said, who came to a tragic end as a fisherman lost at sea. It was a detail that would stick fast in any child's mind. Danny even used to imagine tracking his paternal family down after stumbling on a yellowed eighties news clipping about a boat going down off the south-west coast. For the first six years or so of his life, it was just Danny and his mum. Then there was a new man and a few faintly nomadic years, moving around the borough in their new family unit. It didn't last too long either and it was soon Danny and his mum again. When he first went to school, he did what so many children naturally do and compared himself to his new friends and peers. Why did so many of them have a father figure in their lives when he didn't? But life was too busy, too pressing to be consumed by an unnamed grief. 'When I first started really asking questions, I was just about old enough to get served. I must have been [around] 13 or 14 and I remember going to the shop to get a can of beer and drinking it behind the flats, not that I even felt that morose or whatever, but I thought that was how I should feel and behave in that moment,' he laughed. 'There were times [in my teenage years] when I used it as a justification for being a moody little shit.'

Unlike Jamie, Chloe or myself, it's not as if Danny has any real memories of his father to sustain him or cause pain, at least not of his own. The patchwork he does have comes from the recollections of others: his mum, her close friends and a few of his family members that knew his father, however briefly. It's another thing, having to rely on imagination to fill in the gaps that memory can't. As we talked, I tried to explain how the snatched scraps I have surrounding Christobal sometimes felt more unreal than the figure I'd built for myself over the years, whenever I thought of him at all. It was an explanation that was starting to feel familiar.

A few weeks after my talk with Danny, I'd come across a bundle of papers in a ring binder in my bedroom. It's a collection I'd been carrying about for years, across cities and house shares from Scotland to London. To call it organised would be a generous imaginative flourish. There's little logical structure to its contents, a confusion of old school reports, bank statements, official university correspondence, utility bills and what appear to be a few general scraps of paper that must have once held some kind of significance. What amounts to my entire life in officialese and accumulated rubbish that I've never been able to bear to throw away. An uneven and incomplete paper trail, proof of both long-forgotten days and a reminder of the most vivid. Some of it is priceless. There's a small folder of Mum's illustrations and writing, composed to me as she lay gravely ill in Guy's Hospital. Gently sketched little scenes full of colour and life. Their messages are steady and direct, with a few comic interludes. One traces the outlines of something called the 'Argos Incident', something to do with me and gran getting up to some high jinks at the Catford branch on a hysterical summer afternoon. Gradually, the tone starts to change to something more sombre, an elegy for the happy times we shared and an appeal set against the finality she knew to be coming, right around the corner. Nothing, she wrote, will take away from the love we have had for one another. The rest is and must remain private to me and her alone. Some things aren't for reportage, or any other eyes. A couple of times a year I reread them from start to finish, on some significant date. The anniversary of her passing or birthday, or whenever else I want to feel next to the past.

Not too long after interviewing Danny, I found myself rummaging around the same ring binder, looking for my birth certificate to double check a few details, like the registered addresses both she and Christobal had put down when I was born despite their legal homelessness. What Danny had said about fashioning the information about his own father had struck a nerve. In my searching, I'd found an old school report written by Ms Jackson, my teacher at Fairlawn Primary who became a firm family friend after Mum's death. She had known them both, Mum and Christobal, when the three of us had still lived together in an approximation of a nuclear family unit. It's clear from reading it how Mum's illness had already progressed, which means he must have already been fading out of the picture. 'Francisco has made excellent progress in all areas of the curriculum,' the letter begins. 'I believe this is partly due to the excellent parenting he receives from his mother. His mother always brings him to school on time and is punctual to collect him at the end of the day. Francisco has a great deal of fun with his mother. [She] sensibly wants him to be like all the other children and lead a happy child's life. She is an outstanding parent.' The tone only deviates when it speaks of Christobal and then only briefly, though it sums up so much in so few sentences. 'I have only met Francisco's father on two occasions over the past two years. His English was limited and our conversations were thus brief. He did appear to be quite childlike himself and not [as] mature a parent as his mother.' Still, Ms Jackson had added,

'Francisco's mother is always positive when talking about Francisco's father. She even asked for an extra copy of his report to be sent [to him].'

Danny has his own small private store of physical clues and symbols that have helped build the picture he's constructed of his dad, just like I have the photos and old reports. 'The only thing we really have of his is a stack of old socialist newspapers. I know he liked The Fall and his favourite book was *The Ragged-Trousered Philanthropists*, as well as [bits of] random bureaucracy and paperwork.' I told Danny what he didn't need me confirming – that it was about as consistent a character sketch as you could get for a young man of his dad's era and apparent worldview. 'I'd like to meet him and suss that for myself,' he'd responded. 'A lot of people talk the talk and don't really walk the walk. Did he just have these socialist papers because he was trying to impress my mum or did he really mean it? What would he make of everything going on around us at the moment? There's all these things that I might have inherited from him.' How often, I wanted to know, does Danny think about this obscured part of his own heritage – how much did it mean to him, on a day-to-day basis?

'I think ebbs and flows is the way to describe it. It's something that's always there. Some things set it off. The times where I've wanted to talk to the guy. I was in a very long-term relationship which didn't end particularly well and there were a couple of crunch points when I thought it would be good if there was a bloke there, just to ask what he thinks.' It's strange, Danny said, when he'd spoken to his mum in preparation for our call, she'd told him that his dad had been in a similar long-term relationship before he'd met her. Though a common occurrence, it got Danny thinking: Just how much of his dad's personality had passed on to him? Was history repeating itself? Is he in any way the same person as his father?

'[It's sometimes like] the patterns already there, that things are sort of clicking into place.' These are the thoughts that make the idea of tracking his dad down feel like a priority. 'Other times it's just background noise. Life is busy, you can't be thinking about this all the time. For the Salvation Army application, I'd pieced together a lot from my mum. It felt like an exhaustive process [at the time] though when I look back at it now, it looks a bit threadbare,' Danny added. 'I've had plenty of people ask to my face, why do you even want to find him? It's jarring. Surely it's obvious, even though I sometimes ask what it is I want out of it. It's curiosity more than anything else. What's his hairline saying? What's his accent like? I get half my DNA from him, so it's that curiosity more than anything else [though] maybe it's more than that.'

Danny has his own personal philosophy around the missing. For him, it's always been a two-way bind: the missing and the left-behind, locked together in often mysterious ways. That's what his own life has taught him, at any rate. 'When someone chooses to go missing, people think it's just that person's act, but that isn't it. Everyone left behind them has a person-shaped hole in their lives,' he explained. 'Not long before this phone call, I rang up a friend of mine and it got me thinking. He has a few problems with his mental health and has been in and out of wards for as long as I've known him. We were having a joke the other day by text and he took something I'd said the wrong way. I texted him again and he replied back, 'I don't think we should be friends anymore'. Straight away, I thought: What's going on? We've known each other for years and have never argued about anything, ever. [So I] rang him up and it took him by surprise. He didn't think I'd have reached out, that I'd have just told him to fuck off. He was spoiling for a fight a little bit. Clearly he wasn't in a very good place. I told him that it doesn't work that way. I'm your friend as much as you're my friend, if that makes any sense? You can't just end it like that because you fancy it. You can't just go missing like that, because people will seek you out.'

I'd also wanted to know if anger had ever had anything to do with it. It's a question I told Danny that I'd often asked myself, even though it's an emotion I've never quite explicitly tied on to my thoughts of Christobal. What would be the point? He was, as I fully understood now, just a boy when it had come down to it. Danny told me that no one has ever tried to sugar-coat or hide anything from him, just as no one in my own family had ever done when it came to Christobal. 'My dad being missing made me different to my peers, in a way that I hadn't maybe understood before. The drugs, his absence. That it wasn't something for polite conversation,' Danny said after a short pause. 'You know, that it's not something to shout about. It's not something I'm embarrassed about in any way. But it's more something that people might perceive you as being ashamed of. Does that make sense?' I told Danny it made perfect sense. We were back at the language of missing again. How there was a paucity of communication for the left-behind. 'I think the first real feelings were of anger, yes. That felt natural. [Mum] was always open with me, in as far as you can be open about these things. I don't remember her not wanting to talk about it. You have to remember that she was left behind too, with a child. My grandparents had just moved over to Spain at that point. It was tough for her. Now I can just ring her out the blue and ask a few questions with very little fuss.' That isn't to say that occasional pangs of resentment don't occur. 'Why's my mum been working all this time when this guy has been dossing around living this hedonistic lifestyle? But that's not how it works, is it? If he's knocking about somewhere then [I wonder] what he's thinking. Call it pity or whatever but that could never be me.'

As the weeks passed and life slowly settled into its new rhythms, I found myself lingering on Danny's story more and more. Just like Chloe and Jamie before him, he represented the vast and subtle world of the left-behind. As Daniel put it, things often ebbed and flowed. Sometimes the desire to know felt like one of life's top priorities, even if it usually squatted somewhere just out of reach, stirred into the rest of daily life. There was something else, a vague unease that I struggled to name. Danny had reached out to me as someone who could offer practical advice, some help in his own quest for resolution. But what did I have to offer? I know the truth of it is that I have lived a happy, stable life regardless of the mess that happened to occur in my childhood. I have had opportunities and care. The family I still have may be small and unconventional, but it is tight knit. True, I didn't know too many other people raised by their aunt and elderly grandmother but it wasn't something that ever preyed on my mind. Why would it? What would there even be to consider? One thing about the key facts about the central events of your playing out in extreme youth is that you quickly understand that some things can't be changed. The choice is to fight forward or stare back.

Or maybe that isn't it at all, as smoothly certain as it might sound. There is no roadmap to dealing with grief, whether it's death or the ambiguous loss of the missing. There isn't a template to follow or a library of ideal stock responses with a range of coping systems to slot in depending on the individual. Working through the knots of the past is an often messy and illogical process. Old certainties crumble, new ones are moulded in their place. The events themselves aren't for shifting: they are what they are. What changes is your own relationship to the established facts, the often imperceptible ways that they inform the life you've grown to lead. 'These things [with my dad] happened. It's tough. I mentioned about this relationship I had that ended quite badly. I'm in my mid-20s now and maybe I look back at that with some regret after nine years. But imagine looking back at 30 years of your life with that sensation? The only thing you can do is keep going whatever situation you're in. But it's tough,' Danny repeated. Like Chloe and so many others I'd spoken with, it was impossible to overstate the impact his missing father had had in shaping his life. It was like an explosion. One that you could never quite fully repair, the debris still strewn across both his and his mum's lives. I suppose it applied to me and Christobal, too. Of course there was still a life that had to be led in the here and now. But that didn't mean curiosity had to die, or that the same old questions didn't reassert themselves about the kind of man he was, or might have grown into without me.

A few weeks before my interview with Danny, I'd found myself dialling in to a Skype call with Joe Apps. Things had changed dramatically all those months on from our first meeting at the labyrinthine National Crime Agency offices. After a 15-minute introductory pantomime as the video leered in and out of sound, Joe told me that if work had been busy in the autumn of 2019, then it was something else now. Though I'd long been aware of how little stays still in the world of the disappeared. It was just as true in months after our collective social and working lives had been thrown into disarray. It stood to reason that the missing would hardly be immune. Joe looked and sounded tired, more so than when we'd spoken in the flesh. How was it, tracing missing people from home, I asked. 'Our model runs on giving advice to police forces around searches and forensics or investigative lines of inquiry, so that can be done over the phone,' Joe explained. They've also been using the various tools at their disposal that don't revolve around leaving the house. They can still piece casework together from social media and the genealogy website Find My Past. 'We can use reference documents and things like that. For instance, we're looking for someone on the Isle of Man at the moment. We're finding that by using timetables we can look at where they might have gone and where on the coast they might have hit first. We look through [dead] body finds and other things [like that] and can put out coastal and maritime alerts for neighbouring countries.'

There had also been some resolution on a few stubborn old cases. One was of a woman whose body had been found in Ireland in 1995. She had been wearing French-manufactured shoes and had a set of Volkswagen keys in her possession. 'We looked for the car model and what sort of age it might be. Ok, is it a Polo or a Golf? Then we [looked into] the car and who might have found it.' Eventually, the two physical clues proved enough to go and identify the body. 'There was another case the other day where a body was found with a pair of trainers on. They're only sold in about three outlets in the UK. A quick call around the outlets and a few credit card checks, and we quickly found who the person was, in about half a day. These are the sort of things we can do at a desk,' Joe explained. 'That's going quite well for us, but the major crimes stuff is more difficult. We're having to do case reviews and investigative suggestions over the phone, which never works very well.' The big change was the worry about reporting people missing in the first place and what happened when they came home. 'Have they brought the disease back with them? People are very concerned about how to do stuff and what the best thing to do is.' That counts for police, as well as the missing and the left-behind. 'Policing choices are based on risk. Can we rely on what people in the home are telling us, without having to do a house visit or search? Most often you can.' Another case raised half a smile. There was a young man who had gone missing from Cambridge. 'It was thought he'd gone abroad. A quick look on his Facebook page and he'd documented his whole journey to Paris in photos. After a quick check with the French authorities he was found in prison over there. He was a very easy person to trace.'

At the time we spoke, there had been a crucial change in the make-up of the missing occasioned by the lockdown restrictions, Joe explained. 'Policing has seen a 30 to 35 per cent reduction in missing episodes being reported, while there's an uptick with calls to other services. Some people might not have been coping very well and ring the charities to talk about it. Certainly from a policing perspective, lockdown has seen a marked reduction in the number of reports.' As ever when it came to the figures on the missing, the true picture was slightly more complex than just a straightforward drop. 'We've seen a big uptick in high-risk cases, at about 10 per cent more than there ever have been. Which suggests that there's cause for concern around suicide ideation. It's very worrying. It tells you people are very, very anxious. There are many more bodies being found at the moment. More than we've seen in comparison with other periods over the past couple of years.'

Every day an internal news memo is circulated around Joe's team and, at the time we spoke, every day was seeing more and more bodies discovered. 'People have taken their own lives because they can't cope with life under these restrictions. It's a huge shame,' Joe added with a sigh. After exchanging goodbyes, I put aside the missing for the rest of the day and tried to fill the rest of the day with domestic routines to try and put all of the sadness and desperation out of mind temporarily.

The more I learned about my own past and the stories of others, the more complex the picture became and was still becoming. The weeks drifted into months and I increasingly thought of Danny. It's true, our stories shared some of the same circumstances. Absent fathers whose images we'd fashioned from memory or the memories of others, as well as whatever few physical trinkets we'd happened to accumulate or rediscover over the years. We had both been born in unglamorous parts of London, only a couple of years apart. And here we both stood as two of the left-behind, the details of our lives as broadly similar as anything I'd encountered in my journey through the world of the missing. There were also plenty of differences between us. I realised Danny had taken up the search for his father with more precision than I had with Christobal. He had broadly known what he wanted from it and needed practical advice on how to get to that point. Though his thoughts of his father were anything but straightforward, the desire to know was clear. Danny had been waiting his whole life for those answers that only that knowledge could confer. In truth, I still wasn't quite there yet.

Though Christobal was always in mind as I'd made my way to each homelessness shelter or funeral, from every interview with the formerly missing and the left-behind, I still didn't know what it was I wanted from his memory. But a resolution was on its way, even if I couldn't quite know what form it was going to take yet. The weeks carried on passing. It was interesting, I'd started to note, just how often I was starting to read about La Línea. How much flights would cost, what the weather would be like in the autumn months, where might be a good place to stay in a city that still seemed so alien, even in my daydreams. Danny's desire to know his own father's fate cast the idea of Spain in a new light. Perhaps it really was almost time to return there, after the passage of so many years. Locked down in the middle of a damp British summer, it was hard to picture what it might feel like to loiter on the waterfront there, staring out at the sea and tracing my own faint steps

back into the strange past. But before these thoughts could
be conjured into reality, I had another journey to make into
the world of the left-behind.

CHAPTER 13

The stone-grey skies cast a long shadow indoors as we ordered our coffees from a cheerful waitress at an All Bar One in Newcastle city centre, in the last few days of August 2020. I sat opposite Nick Pope, an avuncular bearded man in his early 50s, who I'd talked to on the phone for ten minutes earlier in the month. Back then, I'd reached out through an intermediary to see if Nick might be interested in an interview about his story. Before agreeing, he'd wanted to know a little more of my intentions and I was more than happy to oblige given the personal, still raw nature of his and his family's story. The bar was a convenient place for us to meet, not too far from where the businessman lives with his wife Andria in Ponteland, a small town in Northumberland about eight miles from Newcastle.

On 28 February 2018, Nick's 19-year-old son Charlie went on a night out in Manchester. He'd only recently left home and had been loving his first year in the city, studying economics and philosophy at the University of Manchester. The night before he'd rang his parents to let them know he was planning to head out with his friends. It was unusually cold out, right in the middle of the Beast from the East cold snap, so they told him to take care in all the snow and ice. Charlie and his friends had done the typical student pre-drinking at their accommodation before heading out into town. They'd made their way to a nightclub called The Zombie Shack on New Wakefield Street, where their evening continued. After leaving the venue, Charlie and his flatmate attempted to board a bus home, but the driver kicked them off for being too drunk. Instead, they decided to make their way back to the club. Back inside, they lost each other somewhere in the crowd and were separated. According to subsequent press reports, Charlie left the venue sometime around 1.20 a.m. and was spotted on CCTV heading back by foot towards his student halls in Fallowfield, about three miles south of the city centre. The next three hours are a blank spot. Charlie was spotted again at 4.43 a.m. making his way back in the direction of the centre of town before making his way down onto the canal towpath by Rain Bar, a gastropub a few streets away from Manchester Oxford Road train station.

The next day brought another phone call for Nick, this time from Charlie's flatmates. He hadn't come home and they were worried about his whereabouts. Nick decided to report him missing straight away. Something was wrong, Nick could feel it in his gut. Manchester city centre is full of canals, built during the Industrial Revolution and abandoned to decline during the latter half of the twentieth century. The last decade or so has witnessed their resurgence, with millions of pounds of investment pumped in to give the derelict old waterways a new lease of life as a crucial part of Manchester's 'regenerated' future. The narrow, winding urban canals that had been filled in only decades before were hastily dredged again, to give birth to new developments with names like New Islington and Piccadilly Village. A cluster of smart bars and restaurants now use the water as a selling point, a charming backdrop to entice drinkers and revellers with a bit of money to spare. Though a frontispiece of the bold new Manchester, maintenance of the old Victorian waterways can be a challenge. In 2013, the responsibility passed from public sector quango British Waterways to a newly established charity, the Canal & River Trust, who have access to a steady stream of funds to make sure things don't slip into disrepair. Nick Pope didn't know much about any of this history when he reported Charlie missing the day after he hadn't returned home from his night out on 28 February. Nor did he know about the darker stories attached to the water, which didn't tend to get carried in enthusiastic press reports about Manchester's gleaming new future. Between 2008 and 2014, over 80 bodies were pulled from canals in the city, the majority of them male. The rate was so high that some speculated about a serial killer at large, a baseless rumour that police had consistently been forced to shut down over the years.

After two terrible days of uncertainty, Charlie's body was found by Lock 89 of Rochdale canal by North West

Underwater Search and Marine officers not far from Rain Bar, on 2 March 2018. He had fallen in and experienced cold water shock, as established by the pathologist at the later inquest. The Pope family had been thrust into the depths of barely comprehensible grief. Later, when Nick was taken to the spot where Charlie had been found, he 'couldn't believe how dangerous it was', he told me as our lattes arrived. It didn't seem to make any sense, just how little protection there was along the water. There were no barriers, or protective equipment, nothing that would break anyone's fall into the canal. Not long after, Nick was made aware of a Change.org petition demanding better protection by the water that had been started by Alona Ainsworth, a young woman from Salford who had read of Charlie's story in the local press. Though she hadn't known the Pope family, the news had hit her hard. 'She was so sick and tired of bodies being pulled out the canal. I found this out later, but she said that she'd been hearing it all her life at least once a quarter. There were about 3000 signatures. I eventually got hold of her about a week or so later. By that point it was up to 10,000. Within weeks that was 30,000.' Some of the stories shared on the petition were powerful, Nick said, which now runs to almost 100,000 signatures. There were messages of support and encouragement, as well as the testimony of those left behind by others that had fallen. People's brothers, sisters and parents who had lost their loved ones over the years and wanted – needed – things to change for the better. Even now, Nick's voice carried a note of incredulity as he asked me, 'How can you sit on that as a city for so long and not do anything about it?'

The tragedy that hit the Pope family is not unique and nor is it just the story of Manchester alone. Months before I'd met Nick in Newcastle, I'd read a report called *Men Missing on a Night Out* by Geoff Newiss and Dr Ian Greatbatch, published in 2017 by the University of Portsmouth's Centre for the Study of Missing Persons. It looked at 96 fatal disappearances of men who had last been seen after a night of drinking, in towns across the country. When Newiss had worked at Missing People back in 2011, he'd noticed a pattern in missing persons reports that showed a significant number of young men out in pubs, bars or clubs who were reported missing after not making it home and were later found dead. Between 2010 and 2018, it was reported that there had been 150 fatal cases of people going missing after a night out, the majority being young men under the age of 35. Of that figure 85 per cent are later found in water,[28] according to the available data. It's thought there are between 10 and 20 such cases every year, with just under half of those involved under the age of 21 and a third being students, like Charlie Pope. Winter accounted for over half of all cases, when the temperature plummets and the risk of cold shock increases. There are the places that become hotspots, where proximity to the water's edge mixes with nightlife. Manchester, Bath, Bristol, Durham, York, Shrewsbury. Each with its own river or canal system, each with its own issue with men going missing after a night out. The chances of them coming home alive are slim.

Both Nick and I had drained our cups quickly, as he told me about what he'd achieved to provoke changes around these grim statistics. From the first months of 2018, he had thrown himself into campaigning for improved water safety, first in Manchester and then beyond. Back then, it felt like one of the only things he could do. After the petition took off, things moved quickly. What could be done, here and now, to stop more needless deaths by the water? Nick wouldn't let it rest. As the petition grew, he launched himself into a campaign to improve safety on the canals. He badgered the relevant authorities for meetings and took to social media. By the end of 2018, an independent safety review commissioned by the Manchester Water Safety Partnership proposed a raft of changes, including awareness programmes and an action plan for the provision of safety equipment. Permanent barriers were installed at Lock 89, as well as better lighting and fencing across the waterways. Practical, common-sense changes to what had seemed an issue of obvious and glaring need.

No, it wasn't unique to Manchester, but the high number of deaths related to its waterways was still the city's problem to deal with. The campaign hadn't always been easy, Nick explained. There had been difficulties at the start, trying to get all the relevant agencies to open their eyes to the scale and severity of the issue. With hindsight, he thinks that there were a few things that contributed to their reluctance. 'If it happened all at once then [it] couldn't be ignored, but because it was spread out over [all] those years, it was different.' Nick also suspects some were frightened of the potential blame and responsibility. There were exceptions. David Wilson stood out. The Greater Manchester Fire and Rescue Service's Station Manager had chaired the water-safety partnership in Manchester and quickly became a close ally in Nick's campaign. 'He'd be the first to admit [the safety partnership] had been fairly ineffectual. After Charlie, when I kicked off about it and the petition started, Dave bought into it from day one. He said he'd do anything he could to help. It was quite political as well. The partnership was composed of the city council, the fire brigade, the police, local business, the waterways owners and the Canal & River Trust.' For Nick, it had started off with a simple focus, more barriers and protection 'for people who might be in a bad way from falling in,' he continued. 'I was focussed on Charlie and young men, but the amount of homeless people that have drowned in there is incredible. I was asked [later] for my help then to get involved in the campaign, to stop people going missing on a night out. There were some great straplines. "Look After Your Mates", "Don't Be the One Left Behind" [and] a few others.' The idea was to get into the minds of students who, like Charlie, were at risk without even knowing it. Nick made a video with the Canal & River Trust, who paid for it to be shot in Manchester. When the students saw it, a hush descended on the room. Coming from Nick, it had a power other appeals couldn't muster. Young men can be reckless. It's part of the deal at that strange time of life, the interregnum between adolescence and adulthood that I'd thought about before I met Jamie in Edinburgh and its relation to our prior lives in Dundee. That unspoken sense of youthful invincibility, until something happened to show it up as the nonsense it always had been.

At the end of 2019, Nick had attended a national water safety conference in London. David Wilson was invited to give a speech from the perspective of the Manchester Water Safety Partnership to representatives from cities all across the UK. 'It was about sharing ideas and best practice, it's really good. Dave's presentation was phenomenal. About how everything was ticking along ok until, and he clicked the next slide, "this happened" and then the world changed.' It was a picture of Charlie. 'He said that all too often we speak about statistics and numbers. It's not about numbers, it's about families and people. It had become personal after he'd been to Charlie's funeral and got to know us as a family.' The slide after was a picture of the entire Pope family, Charlie included, outside their home. You could hear a pin drop, Nick added. 'I got up and did a bit about what it meant to us and why we've done what we've done. The vast majority of people who were in there were passion-ate campaigners but they hadn't lost anyone. I said I can't believe how good you guys are. It's easy for me as it's so personal. So please, if you're having a bad day and can't get the right people in the room, then don't give up.' Of all the things Nick told me, I couldn't stop these words reverberating around my head when I later sat down to write them up. The force of his campaigning and its tangible successes spoke to Nick's nature, as well as the power of the left-behind. What he'd said made me reconsider some of the people I'd met before Nick, from all over the world of the missing. The people who searched and advocated for those who had fallen from sight, without anything to animate them other than the fact of it being the right thing to do. But without Nick's relentless drive, it felt like the particular campaign to improve Manchester's water safety wouldn't have been anything like as successful. At the start, it had needed him and the focus brought by his grief. It had a simple, unignorable goal: no more avoidable deaths and no more lives lost when the costs of change amounted to so little.

As we'd carried on talking, I heard from Nick a variant of the same thing I'd heard from so many on my journey through the world of the missing and that I knew something about from my own experiences with Mum and Chritsobal. That there is a life before and a life after the event itself. From Jamie and Daniel, who had been left behind in their different ways with their respective parents, to Esther and all of the returning missing, life was different now. Not in some vague and ill-defined way like the inevitability of one year feeling different from the next, but something permanent, which no amount of grief or understanding of that grief could change.

There's a man in Nick's town who he often bumps into when he's out walking his dog. They'd never spoken until the man came up to him to ask how he was getting on with the work on the Manchester canals. 'I hadn't realised he was a Manc originally. He'd grown up there and said how lethal those canals were 40, 50 years ago. We all knew, he said. The ones that were switched on avoided them. That was part of my point [with raising awareness]. Charlie didn't know the city before he went to university. He didn't have a clue how dangerous it was.'

I asked Nick if there were ever any points when he was shocked at the level of support and kindness that poured out after he lost his son. There had been times when it had surprised him, he replied. The petition was evidence of that and just how many others were living in the aftermath of similar stories. It was so sad, he continued, to hear the news from Manchester just a few months after Charlie's passing. Another 19-year-old, Orlando Nyero, was found around 30 yards from where Charlie had been, on the very same strip of canal. 'It was the same story, the whole lot. He was a student at Wolverhampton back home for the weekend. They'd been out and they fished him out a few days later. Dave [Wilson] rang me up, bless him, to let me know. He was in tears on the phone. That was another warning that this would just keep happening. The petition jumped off the scale after that.' Though social media showed the best of people, it could also contain its fair share of cruelty. Just like its use in the search for the missing, it wasn't always clear what you would get. 'It certainly opened my eyes to online trolling. It was people saying, oh the canals have been there for 200 years, start telling these kids to stop getting pissed and everything will be fine. I was very conscious the whole way through not to criticise Manchester or the people there. As I said, Charlie loved it, he was having a blast. Yes, the canals have been there for centuries but the bars and restaurants haven't. How about putting some protection in there?' It isn't the only city that can feel like it's changed beyond recognition. At the start, I'd mentioned how I'd stayed not far from Newcastle's recently trendified Quayside on my previous solo visit on my way up to Dundee, a month or so prior. 'It's funny you said that,' Nick added. 'It was a total no-go zone when I was a kid. None of those bars were there. It was a dangerous derelict place with no [protection] by the water. Look at how safe it is now. There's plenty of stuff, barriers and rings. My friend Tommy is a firefighter and he told me he does a lot of water-safety training with the bars there. The bouncers are trained to throw ropes and they've saved five lives there over the past 18 months. They're doing that in Manchester now. It's really come on.'

Time did strange things that first year after Charlie's passing. Sometimes it didn't feel possible that many months could have elapsed, though it could also feel never ending. On 1 March 2019, it felt like Nick and his family had needed to plan something to try and turn some of the agony into something positive. Charlie had been known for his generosity; it's just the sort of person he'd been. That's how 'Charlie's Good Deed Day' was born. It was simple, with the family encouraging people on the day to perform a random act of kindness, it didn't really matter what it was. 'A simple gesture that will make someone smile is all that's required, be it a bunch of flowers, holding a door open for someone, carrying their shopping to the car. Just tell them why you are doing it by mentioning Charlie's Good Deed Day,' the family said in a statement. 'Charlie was a very generous and giving young man and always a joker, so for people to smile in his memory would make him so proud.' It didn't take long for the idea to take off, far beyond what Nick or his family had ever envisaged. 'We did it on the first and again this year for the second anniversary. It was brilliant actually. It was my wife's idea. Anniversaries are hard, but the worst is the one of his death. We were coming up to it and we were trying to think, Well, what do we do? Some good advice I was given was to always make a plan. Don't just get there without [one], it's too distressing like that. Someone said, why not random acts of kindness? After that, it became Charlie's Good Deed Day.' A friend had printed business cards and distributed them and a Facebook page was created, which quickly garnered hundreds of followers posting their own small acts of charity. The first anniversary had fallen on a Friday and some of Charlie's friends contacted Nick, asking if they could have a get-together in the local pub, the same one where they'd held the wake a year earlier. 'There were hundreds of them there, all coming up to me to tell me about their good deed. I was wowed. That's when we decided to do it every year.' I told Nick it sounded like Charlie had an amazing bunch of friends, which he assented to with a vigorous nod. At the funeral itself a year before, the family had tried to keep things as light as possible, with everyone in bright colours, talking about Charlie's life. For a number of the younger attendees, it might have been their first experience of a major bereavement. 'They might not have lost anyone and certainly not anybody that young. Some of his mates had bought a load of yellow balloons, with cards tied to them so that people could write a message on them. After the funeral we went off to bury Charlie and they set them off into the sky. It was a really nice touch.'

Right at the end of our talk, Nick told me about the night before the call to tell them Charlie hadn't come home, when the weather had been at its worst, with the storm raging outside. Nick and Andria were at the family home, sitting with the fire on, watching TV with the dog and cat milling about the room. 'Charlie was having a great time in Manchester, his older brother was having a great time in Leeds, and Daisy was out with her boyfriend. We have three healthy kids and we're sitting with our pets in our nice warm house. A lot of people don't have that. We said to each other that we need to appreciate how lucky we are.' The next day, Nick continued, their world exploded. Still, he told me that he considers himself to be a fortunate person. 'We've still said since that we're lucky. Something terrible has happened to us. But compared to most people, we are still very lucky.' That night was the last of their old life, the time before their loss and everything that has happened since. 'You reflect on that [evening] and it is the happiest we are ever going to be. It's never going to get better than that. We'll manage to live with this, but it numbs you to joy. It's strange that it should be that particular night [before Charlie went missing]. You have to live the new normal. The old one is gone and it isn't ever coming back.'

The mosaic of the missing I'd created looked different from this new perspective, after my afternoon with Nick. It was as if some of the more jagged pieces started to slip into place. In the days after, I poured over everything from my first meeting with Joe Apps when he'd patiently explained to me the outline of the numbers behind the missing persons crisis, right through my work into all the ways that people were vanishing and some of the circumstances that led them to slide from view. I reread and listened over my interviews with the people I'd met at Crisis at Christmas in the temporarily converted school in north London, who had spent time living on the streets and flitting from sofa to sofa at the mercy of friends and their exhaustible stores of patience. I went through the reports I'd read on the crumbling, heavily privatised world of children's homes. Missing children and the adults on the margins of society, clinging on by the diligence of charities and frontline workers, who occasionally seemed to be hanging on themselves, working impossible hours to stem the rising tide of vulnerability. I thought about county lines and the teenagers far from home, their lives stripped down to a life of shifts selling heroin and crack. Then there were the victims of modern slavery, brought to the UK from Eastern Europe or South East Asia, to name just two examples, with the promise of a new start, only for the dream to shift into a nightmare when they found themselves enslaved and repressed from sight. Their captors had gambled that no one would notice, or perhaps even care, about their absence. How many thousands of people were living with the facts of their very existence cut out from under them? It was impossible to say, just like the 'real' overall number of missing people and the untold number who are never recorded or become a statistic.

If I understood anything, it was that missing wasn't just about statistics and how to record them. It was about the individual lives and stories of the missing themselves and the left-behind. Something about our society seemed to make the process of falling out of sight appear easier than ever. One day you can be here and the next you might be gone. But missing itself is not the disease. It doesn't happen in a vacuum, all by itself. There are factors that make your disappearance more or less likely. Poverty, mental health, debt, family breakdown, addiction, the violence of others. The support that used to exist is harder to come by than it was. This erosion of the social safety net was not an inevitability. It had been brought on by ideology and apathy. There is a clear and obvious solution to this side of the story of the missing. More funding for mental health services, the building of affordable housing, provision of properly regulated children's homes in the areas of the country that need it the most. Money to match the easy sentiments. How prevention is crucial. That something had to get better in attending to the return, which is what most missing people do. There is a moment to grasp, to understand exactly what has led someone to disappear and to stop it from occurring again. It is not always linear or straightforward.

Of course, the missing are not unique to our time and place. People have vanished all over the world for as long as there have been places to vanish from. If someone has not been taken, or is an adult with the capacity to make their own decisions without a history of pressing vulnerability in their life, then going missing can be a choice. Or it could be something bigger and more profound than that. The right to be forgotten, to get up and walk away from one kind of life and stride forward into the new.

There was something else that I was surer of. When I'd met Jamie Reid in Edinburgh and Nick Pope in Newcastle, they had mentioned the support of those around them, loved ones and friends, to keep them going in their darkest days in the shadow of their missing. There were people in their lives who had rallied round and tried their best to cushion some of the blow. As much as the broader safety net desperately needs to be repaired and bolstered, I couldn't stop thinking about something else that could begin much closer to home in the fight to bring the missing, or those perilously at risk, from falling any further from vision. We all have a responsibility to ourselves and others. This is not a crisis that is only real for other people. The missing are not a separate group, divorced from the fabric of the world. They are not an abstraction. They could be your brother, husband or friend. Most of us are occasionally guilty of averting our eyes from the things that frighten us or seem too impossibly large to solve by individual acts of kindness or generosity. This is not a sermon. I have spent much of my own life entangled with my thoughts of Christobal and the story of the missing. And yet, there have been times when I knew I could have done more to stop a descent I could see playing out before my eyes. The friends that needed more help than I could give, the good not done from laziness or embarrassment. Would it take so much for any of us to pick up on the signs and act? What would it take to support the people in our lives that we know are struggling with any of the innumerable things that lead a person to disappear? As Caroline Haughey, the lawyer who has given so much of her working life to the fight against modern slavery, had told me, it is all connected. And it is more than that. We are all connected, the missing and the rest of us, left behind. We share the same spaces, fears and anxieties. They are us, just we could be them at any time.

The couple of weeks that had passed after my afternoon with Nick Pope in Newcastle had been spent in what had become my typical 2020 routine. I'd meet people whose lives had been touched by the missing and I'd speak with them for as long as they were happy to tell me their story. They could be those like Nick who had lost family and lived now with his loss, who had given up something of his life since to try and make sure no one else had to get hit with the pain they'd experienced. Or like my old friend Jamie Reid, who had spent all those months back in 2014 waiting for news of his mother's fate. After the interviews, I would sit and listen back, setting their words down, reading around what they told me and trying to write something as faithful to their stories as possible. You try to do your best by people. If they had given me their time and shared their griefs then it seemed obvious that it was the only available option; anything less would be a betrayal. I read over my notes and cross-checked details online. It could often feel strange, moving the pieces around, trying to set them beside each other to build a story that stretched across individuals into something that was supposed to cohere into a patch-work that spoke to the wider story of the missing persons crisis. Nick had taken his tragedy and thrown himself into campaigning for better water safety. Jamie had taken his mum's loss and channelled some of his energy into a new life, a career as a social worker that was going from strength to strength. I knew, and they didn't need me to explain, that it wasn't the whole picture. But what did that mean? Their losses weren't a balance sheet, to be divided up and weighed between the good and bad that had come from them. Life had to go on; there wasn't another option. They all had other people who depended on them in the here and now. The loved ones left behind with them, doing their best in this new chapter of their lives together after the pain they'd lived through.

It wasn't long after meeting Nick that I booked my flight out to Spain, for mid-September. The moment itself was ordinary enough. I brought out my debit card and paid for the flights online, before booking a few nights' worth of basic accommodation in Seville and, finally, a coach to La Línea. It hadn't been any one thing that had finally pushed me into action, but a slow accumulation of encounters. My discussions with the missing and left-behind. Conversations with my own friends and family. The morning thoughts that come with manic clarity after a poor night's sleep. After so many months spent making my way around the UK, in search of the missing, there was an irrational voice that relished the kind of novelty it seemed to represent. The glee of feeling like the whole enterprise was building to a logical ending, that Christobal was just about in sight now. There was still a part of me that fixated on finding the answer, as if this was a problem that could be solved by simple revision and study. But I knew that this homecoming of sorts wasn't going to be as straightforward as that occasionally useful delusion would have it. The weeks before my flight continued to pass by smoothly, as the days passed into night. I started to sleep better and it was odd to note how often my dreams were beginning to fill with the Rock of Gibraltar.

PART VI
THE END OF THE LINE

CHAPTER 14

The middle-aged man behind the counter at the tobacco shop a few yards from Catedral de Sevilla had been incredulous, his eyes creased into laughter behind his disposable mask. Alright, he had a point, even if it was one I'd heard more than a few times before. We'd started out on more solid footing a few seconds before, as I'd walked into the shop to escape from the midday sun. I'd almost been flattered when he'd gestured for me to show some ID before he'd hand over my cigarettes, a request I'd last heard about a decade ago in the UK. After fumbling for my passport and pulling down my own mask, he'd seen my name and sent a volley of conspiratorial Spanish straight back in exchange. Seeing my face drop into strained incomprehension was when the laughter started. 'No español?' he said, rocking his head from side to side. 'No, no Spanish,' I smiled back with a few traces of red breaking out across my face.

It's been the case for as long as I can really remember. How can a Francisco Garcia-Ferrera have red hair, an indeterminate London accent and not even the good sense to have a few words of conversational Spanish? It's a sorry enough state of affairs back home, let alone in Andalusia. It's true, I don't look or sound anything like my name and never have done, facts that hardly matter past a few casual remarks from new acquaintances in London or wherever I happen to find myself in the UK for work or leisure. The brief, confused encounter with the man handing over my pack of cheap Spanish tobacco was the first of its kind I'd experienced after touching down in Seville at the start of my trip to Andalusia. Finally, in the middle of September of 2020, I'd arrived on the last stretch of my journey into the world of the missing and my own reckoning with the past. On the flight over, I'd felt the excitement building into an almost childish restlessness. The night before, I'd packed my small suitcase with an almost comical fastidiousness and forensic attention to all the wrong details. With far too many books for a week and two freshly purchased bottles of sunscreen, it looked like what it was: the bag of a man who didn't really know too much about where he was going and what he expected to find there, beyond the promise of the guidebooks I'd read and the advice I'd solicited from friends who knew the region.

After everything else in my search for Christobal and for the rest of the missing in the UK, it felt like the only natural place to end and reflect on the years and months that had passed in my writing and reporting on the subject. But I knew it was to stand for something more than that too. It was the conclusion of something wider that had spanned more time than the course of writing this book alone. Twenty years, that's how long it had been since that last time I'd set foot in Andalusia as an eight-year-old on that confused, sometimes tense trip to La Línea not long after Mum had died. This wasn't just 'work' in some abstract sense. This was the history of my entire life. Having lived for so many years as an unconvincing-looking and sounding Francisco Garcia-Ferrera, it felt like this was the best chance I'd ever encounter to legitimise the 'Spanish half' of me and make some final sense of my journey through the missing towards Christobal.

I'd been thinking about that long ago visit as the minicab weaved out of the gentle early Monday-morning traffic, from south-east London to Stansted Airport. There wasn't too much to remember, as I sat in the back seat trying to be honest with myself. So much time and so many events had happened in the intervening years. All the new chapters and false starts. The few blurred impressions that came back were just that, fleeting bits of clarity against a shifting backdrop. Tall white buildings and untroubled blue sea on the coastline. An afternoon over the border in Gibraltar and the slapstick arrival of an irate monkey, the territory's principal tourist trap, slapping my lunch out of my hand. And there was Christobal, his skin further yellowed, his body almost bent in on itself. He didn't look good. Worse, he seemed to be fading away, I can remember thinking to myself, even then. Something had changed, or perhaps it had always been there, unnoticed through my infant eyes.

Less a man and more of a sickly child swamped in adult clothing.

Before Mum's death, I'd already known that he didn't behave like other people's idea of a father, but it was worse than that in La Línea. It had been an anxious, raw time back home and that atmosphere had naturally come with me to Spain. It's not to say there aren't other happy little vignettes from the trip, playing the first *Gran Turismo* on my uncle David's PlayStation, having him take me for a short drive on his moped, watching the boats drift lazily along the horizon under the afternoon sun. Further brief flashes of sense and touch and smell. Aunts and distant cousins talking in voluble Spanish, at breakneck speed. A few chaotic market-stall scenes and the strange comforts of a foreign supermarket, full of half-familiar goods displayed in too bright colours and what I could only understand as an alien language.

The last few days before my trip to Spain had passed without too much anxiety. On the Saturday before my flight, my partner had turned 30. It was a joyous day, with any thought of the missing and Christobal pushed temporarily out of mind. There had been a small party that had gone on until the early hours. The Sunday after drifted by in a kind of haze, the main goal being to try and get back to the right mental and physical condition to brave the prospect of the Ryanair flight to come. It had been a long year, with the effects of the pandemic and my saturation with Christobal and the missing having taken its toll. It was rare to be in a house with some of my loved ones and felt good to get wrapped up in giddiness and celebration for a brief few hours.

It was hot as I arrived at the airport, with the last few traces of Indian summer still in the air. Before heading inside the terminal, I double- and triple-checked my bags for essentials out of nerves rather than precision. If it had been a long time since my last visit to southern Spain, then the year of working on the book had made it feel longer still. It was like the more I'd read of Christobal, the further away it seemed to recede from view. The airport was quiet inside, the usual crush of travellers jostling into security lines replaced by a slow trickle of masked-up tourists on their way to only they knew what. I'd arrived early, too early, so I took myself to one of the open-plan cafes and sat staring out at the runway tarmac over a coffee until my flight number flashed for boarding on the electronic screens overhead.

I've never thought about Spain as being my country, in the same way I've never really known how to sum up my relationship with Christobal. Did I abandon this part of my heritage or was it always something more passive than that, a tacit understanding that it might all just be for the best? After touching down in Seville, I was greeted by a wall of dazzling afternoon light and hailed a taxi to take me the 20 minutes or so into town, greedily drinking in the unfamiliar billboards in Spanish and the steady drip of suburbs that were quickly subsumed by the picturesque narrowness of the city centre.

On the back seat, I daydreamed about Mum and a few flashes about Christobal. How she'd maybe taken the same route in on one of her own visits to a city she'd loved. Having dropped my bags off and quickly showered, it was time to take myself out. There was a decent breeze underneath the afternoon heat and I started laughing to myself the first time I paused for a drink and something to eat in a sun-dappled square, at just how easy it was to get lost in reverie and struck dumb with the sense of how absurd it all felt. And just how different it all was from the picture I'd drawn in my mind. The divergences weren't always physical. The streets were just as thin as I'd imagined and just as crammed with centuries of conflicted tradition, a dizzying mix of Moorish style and Catholic bombast. The colours were brighter than home, the social life of the city more immediately and obviously cross-generational. I'd watched grizzled old men with thousand-yard stares as they played cards and gossiped like fishwives and, later, as young families as they settled down to their leisurely evening meals that seemed to spool out for hours. Things started and finished later. That first night, I took myself out for an evening walk, letting my feet guide me without much of a plan. It was better that way, I told myself. There was still a bit of that cooped-up energy in my legs.

It was still early evening and the streets were quiet, save for a few of the more committed mid-afternoon drinkers who had lingered on and would likely power straight through until the early hours. The sky was cloudless, the late September heat more bearable than I'd planned for. I needed to uncoil and walk off some of the nervous energy I'd felt collecting after my arrival in Andalusia for over two decades. After about an hour and a half, my pace slackened as the first injection of adrenaline and novelty started to wear off. Eventually, I found a little bar called La Jeronima about 20 minutes from my accommodation which my perfunctory online search told me was a good place to stop for a quiet read and restorative drink. I'd arrived early by Spanish standards, not long after 7 p.m., and watched as it gradually filled up with young, earnest-looking types who settled into immediate, heated discussion at the tables around me. Though it was always likely to be fantasy, I'd thought I'd have felt something more, at least a kindling of inherited familiarity if nothing else. Wasn't this one of the cities that Mum had fallen in love on her first trips over to Spain? Shouldn't I feel some sort of shock of recognition here? On the way back to my studio apartment I stopped for a final drink and watched some of the life around me, quite enjoying the sense of the night folding out into itself for the people around me, who were entirely oblivious to my existence.

As I got ready for bed, the sound of footsteps outside grew fainter and sparser as the shadows tripped up and down the wall and I lay awake until the early hours. From that first night in Seville, I resolved to keep myself to myself for the few days I had in a city that soon felt it had been purpose built for the kind of trip I'd chosen it for. It wasn't anything like I'd experienced earlier, in my other trips to slightly unfamiliar parts of the UK. In Newcastle or Manchester, I was only ever a few easy hours away from home. When I'd met with Esther Beadle or Hendrix and Hannah at Coffee4Craig the hours would melt past and there would be a train back to London at the end of it, a full stop on the day and the chance to digest some of what I'd heard from them about their own stories or the people they worked with. In Seville and without the normal distractions of my life, there wasn't any other choice but to confront the past I'd come to finally confront, head-on.

It was a fine early morning as I packed up my things and left for the coach station in Seville for my 9.30 a.m. bus to La Línea. The sky was a brilliant pink and I'd arrived early enough for a coffee and a cigarette before departure. Seville had helped me to get my thoughts in order as the clock ticked down for my final journey, right into the heart of Christobal's home city. It was a different kind of excitement that morning as I boarded the coach, alongside my ten or so fellow passengers. A slightly nervous sense of anticipation for something I'd been building towards over the months with the missing, all of the long and uneven years I'd spent thinking of Christobal, and exactly what it was that he meant to me. This was it. This was real, I thought to myself as the coach pulled out of the station and propelled on to the highway south.

For the next four hours, I sat with a book unopened on my lap, gazing out as the landscape shifted and a few of my fellow travellers spoke in hushed indoor voices. Middling-sized apartment blocks in terracotta or baby blue melted past. There was an end-of-the-line feeling to the journey and not just because of my own history and where I was in my work with the missing. It is, quite literally, a trip to the end of the line, as far as the southern tip of Spain goes before the geopolitical absurdity of Gibraltar and the northern coastline of Morocco. At every town and stop along the way, the relative polish and obvious liveliness of Seville receded further and further from view. Each new bus terminal and out-of-the-way town seemed to be smaller and more barren than the last. The land grew arid and rocky, as the number of passengers on the coach started to dwindle until it was just me and an excitable middle-aged man on the front seats, who appeared to be making a private sport of trying, and failing, to engage the driver in animated conversation. As we hit the outskirts of La Línea we passed large detached houses and more soft pastel-coloured apartment blocks, which gave way to 24-hour cafes in crumbling retail units, empty car dealerships and exasperated furniture stores that had seen brighter days. It looked more like New Jersey than what I thought I'd started to know about Andalusia from my days in Seville.

A few things began to stir faintly in my memory as we pulled into the rundown old bus station a few hundred yards from the coastline. I fancied that this or that spot looked half familiar, a dim relic from my only other previous trip as an eight-year-old. In truth, I felt like a fraud on arrival in La Línea. Like a spy sent on a terrible covert mission to seek out a version of my past that might just have been better off left alone. I wondered if the locals in town could see through me at first glance. That I didn't really belong here as anything other than a jumped-up tourist with vague notions of his own tangled, mostly forgotten past. As I'd dragged myself from the worn-out bus station and up the couple of miles of coastline to my odd little 12th-floor Airbnb, it all felt wrong. My layers of clothes and prissy suitcase with the jammed back wheel that caused it to shriek against the slightest movement. I'd thought about hailing a cab, but I couldn't find one and didn't fancy lugging my belongings around the backstreets on what had the premonition of a futile search. After 40 minutes in a straight line up the coast, I'd arrived to be handed my keys by a concierge whose bearing suggested a vast and private mischief. The lift up to the apartment groaned and whistled before I arrived at the 12th floor and turned the key in the lock. After dropping my bags I went out to the balcony, which backed onto an unbroken view of the sea and the entire strip I'd walked down earlier in the day, as well as Gibraltar, looming against the skyline.

I fussed around my cramped apartment and thought about where the day might take me. This was different from Seville. This was where the whole of my journey had been pointing, ever since that first visit to the National Crime Agency offices in Vauxhall all those months before. The place where Mum and Christobal had met and fallen in love. The city where I'd last seen him all those years ago. There was a light mist on the air and a gentle threat of rain. The main strip in town was a few miles away, so I packed my bag and explored my more immediate surroundings. After an hour walking up a deserted dust trail I thought it best to turn back as a few men on mopeds stopped to take a closer inspection at an obviously lost-looking tourist. The evening was drawing in as I sat back on the balcony, trying to think of something to occupy myself with. Restlessness and boredom – these weren't what I had come for. These were supposed to be the hours of grand revelation, where all of the pieces would slide together in perfect harmony. When I would be able to stride down into the centre of La Línea and declare to myself that the past made sense. The epiphany hours, when everything would slot seamlessly into place and all of the endless confusion would dissipate.

There was something I had to admit to myself. I was tired. My body felt unnaturally heavy, dragged down by the unfamiliar humidity and the earlier slog from the bus station. But my mind was something, somewhere, else. My thoughts were so light, I could feel them tripping over one another in their race for attention. I was really here. This was really me, sitting here 12 floors in the sky, looking over the palm trees and speckled little buildings below. Those were real people dotted across the thin streets, running along the groove of their daily lives. So many thoughts and so little time. What had I really come here for and would I know it if I saw it? If I saw him? I looked through the photos I'd brought with me, including one of me, Christobal and a few members of my extended family taken on that last trip in 2000, each face looking slightly more dazed than the last. There were only 60,000 people in La Línea, I reasoned, so it wasn't unlikely that someone would know them if I did decide to ask a few questions and finally dig down into the question of his fate.

But there was another voice inside me, one that I'd heard in the weeks before my trip and that had been growing louder during my days in Spain. After all of the long months and years in my journey towards Christobal and the missing, there was still so much I didn't know. Sometimes it was an ignorance that came from choice. Now, in La Línea, I realised there was a limit to how much I actually wanted to play the role of detective in my past. The knowledge of all the history that might be better left undisturbed. As I looked around the odd if faintly anonymous Airbnb, I knew with growing certainty that I wasn't going to seek him out, or any other Garcia-Ferrera who might still call the city home. At this proximity to him, the idea of reconnection suddenly felt absurd. I didn't belong here in any meaningful way. It wasn't just nerves that I felt, but homesickness too. Nothing in La Línea made much sense yet and I wasn't sure how much energy I had left to change that fact. I didn't recognise anything about myself in this city. It wasn't shameful that I'd expected something to ring louder inside me when I'd had a chance to put my feet on the concrete here. That something would inevitably click and make sense of the days I was going to spend here, chasing his memory and visions of my own half-forgotten childhood. But instead, it all felt more alien than ever. In La Línea, there was no pretence of being anything else than alone with all the disappointments of the past. I looked at the picture again. And there I was, the little boy who the years would have changed beyond recognition. Embarrassment, that's what I felt. The idea of turning up unannounced as a 28-year-old man, demanding an explanation of long-ago mistakes and deeply buried pain. It took coming all the way to La Línea to know that I wasn't capable of dropping that bomb on my – or his – life and easily dealing with the consequences as they inevitably fanned out from my actions. And this was my decision and my life; no one else had the right to live it for me. Being here was enough to know that whatever else happened it had taken courage to make this trip and to bring myself to this strange little city that embodied all of the most important riddles and confusions of my past. For some, not knowing is the worst kind of hell there is and can ever be. For others, the threat of who you might find is the more terrible thought. The answer seems to hinge on a million, often competing variables. Who you are and the places you happen to find yourself in. After all of the months with the missing, I finally knew which side was home when it came to Christobal.

Part of me was surprised at my own decisiveness. As the sky faded into dark I decided to put these thoughts aside and make the most of the night. An earlier search had brought up one of the time-honoured certainties of the Brit abroad experience. The Liffey is an Irish bar right in the heart of La Línea, about a five-minute walk from the odd little border with Gibraltar. After the days spent by myself in Spain with nothing but the missing for company, I decided that it sounded like the best Thursday night dreamed by any man since the dawn of time. After all the loneliness and absence, I think I just wanted to talk. It took about 45 minutes to get to the bar and was unmistakable when I did. The squat little building next to a kebab shop and facing out to a square dotted with apartment blocks. I ordered a beer and observed my fellow drinkers, a diverse mixture of old and young, men and women, some in work gear and others in smart outfits suitable for a late week-night out. Before long I drummed up a conversation with the man at the next table who was also sitting by himself, looking dreamily out at the water. There was a bit of small talk and then the inevitable question of what I was doing in town. It doesn't matter the language, climate or country, I'd banked on the fact of any pub being full of people who can talk a good game. The Liffey was certainly no exception. As I chatted to Sean, a heavy rain started to fall, casting Gibraltar in a thicker fog that seemed to cut it in half. Like any half-decent journalist, I wanted to know his story. He'd been an optician in Dublin for 15 years before moving out to Spain for a job in the computer-gaming industry, which was apparently thriving in Gibraltar. Like many of the other patrons, he lived in La Línea where housing costs were dramatically cheaper. He liked it here, the weather and food were good and the locals unpretentious. 'Oh no,' he said with a smile, 'I can't imagine the idea of going back home.' Soon enough, the night picked up into something else. We were joined by Angela and her partner Paul, who had lived in La Línea for a few years and knew it like the back of their hands, in a way I took to be quite beyond the typical expat experience. After another beer I explained a bit more of my story and why I was there. Angela told me that there was a shop I could go to, not far from the pub, run by a family who were something of a local legend. 'It's down on what I call the "Boulevard of Broken Dreams",' she said to laughter, pointing across to a string of shop fronts by the border which were dimly illuminated by a few unreliable-looking street lights. On account of the city being the way it was, everyone knew everyone, though they weren't always willing to talk to outsiders. 'But they'll probably know [your family] if they're a La Línea family,' she added. It had been a hard year, she explained, with the stringent Spanish lockdown and everything that had come with it. Angela, who was English, had ended up in the city after years spent in Belfast and a few in London. She loved it here, she told me as Paul came back with another round of drinks. Really, he told me, 'it wasn't any worse than other places, as long as you kept to yourself and didn't go asking for trouble.' The night carried on and our conversation arched out in a hundred different directions. The rain had eventually calmed down as the sky settled into a shade of thick turquoise. Others joined our table and I repeated my story and the purpose of my visit, to a chorus of advice. Aside from the temperature, it could easily have been any pub back home, a cacophony of British and Irish voices, and familiarly branded lager. When I finally got back to the apartment, the wind was up and I lay on my bed, laughing to myself at the idea of my half-Spanish heritage and resolutely English habits.

As the next morning broke, I took myself down the coastline, past the swell of commercial boats and a few fathers and sons out with their fishing lines. In the Saturday sun the sky almost felt like too much, a limitless horizon spreading out in every direction from the bay to the rocks and the jagged hills in the distance. As I walked down to the thin strip of store fronts and palm trees by the border a weak breeze was starting to blow from the south, just enough to dilute the worst of the heat and blow away some of the thick, clammy haze. The steady trickle of people alongside me were old and young, some striding purposefully, on their way to work or some other necessity. Others were relaxed, walking a pace that spoke to formless weekend days spent following your feet to whatever kind of indolence they happen to lead you to. The days that pass without a trace. For so many months, I'd been with the first crowd, all over the UK, keeping appointments with the missing and those in their shadows, or involved in trying to trace them. Countless miles walked, hundreds of trains and buses, on my way to sit and talk and listen, trying to understand something the people lost and what led to their disappearances. Trying to gauge how our society and all we individuals within it could do better to stem and treat the crisis and adequately support the returned as well as the left-behind. As I stood there, on that not quite unfamiliar bit of land, it suddenly all felt so very far away. The narrative points of a life that might as well have belonged to someone else. That's what I was looking for then: answers, solutions, different ways to keep people in sight.

So what was it I was looking for here, along the borderland waterfront? Not for Christobal, as he might appear in the present. Perhaps it was never just about him alone. I'd been waiting for so long to bring myself here and wait for something to jump out and make sense of his – our – story. From the start I'd known that the idea of closure was little more than a pipe dream. Almost everyone I'd met through the missing had told me that already, from Joe Apps to Nick Pope. Life is not a set of plot points, drawn up and mapped out with perfect logic or precision, however much we sometimes wish it might be, if only to breathe some sense into the messiness of the choices we make and all the other things we never had a chance to control. But knowledge isn't hope, just like the missing are never dead and never really alive to us, either. Here and nowhere, their absence serves as a damning rebuke to the imperfect certainties we cling on to so tightly, if only to avoid scaring ourselves and others. I narrowed my eyes to the worst of the heat, though it was starting to fade as I thought about turning back from the water and making my way back to the outer fringes of La Línea. Gibraltar sat there, looming with its full weight over the strange, troubled little city that Christobal and his family have called home for so many generations. I'm not sure how long I'd been standing with my eyes fixed on the vast blueness in front of me, but the silence told me I was almost alone now. If this was it, then it was what I'd come well prepared for. No cosmic realisation, no sudden epiphany, no heightened moment of understanding. It just wasn't that sort of day, as I've come to think I might just not be that sort of person. Before I'd arrived in Spain, I thought it might be fitting to leave a little something, a marker for Christobal and Mum, in what I knew had been a significant place for them in their best days. But I couldn't think of the right gesture. Whatever came to mind felt like too much or too little. Instead, I shut my eyes and tried to remember what their voices had sounded like, though I already knew that none of their traces remained in my mind. The day passed. Back on the 12th floor, I sat on the balcony and watched another night fall over the troubled little city I still couldn't understand, as a few mopeds backfired in the distance and the water stirred, inky black and silent. At a loss, I took out my notebook and wrote the words that came into my head, as clear as the autumn moon which beamed out above me and cast the pages into light:

If I knew you better, there would be so many things I'd like to ask. Forgive me if the questions I do have seem small to you, Dad. I don't want to know why and have no interest in excuses. Too many years have passed for them to make any sense, for me or you. The things I want to know are the things I've never known. The things that no one else can tell me. You are not just a ghost. I want to know about some of the things that made you the person you were. What was it like to grow up here in La Línea? Did you and your brothers ever play in the dust and noise out back from your home? And did you fight with them when they tried your patience, as brothers often do? Did your mum and dad ever scold you for acting out, or did your smile always let you get away with murder? What was it like to live so close to the sea? Did you ever bunk off school to smoke and get up to adolescent nonsense with your friends? What football team did you decide to support and why? What secret dreams came to you when you looked out over the city sky at night? Who was your first love, if you ever had one, before Mum? There are so many more questions, but it might be that these are things that you want to keep to yourself and I'd understand that only too well. It's something we all feel, the fragments to keep close and out of sight to even those who we know the best and love the most.

I'd like to know if you were ever scared. I know that some fathers wouldn't like to admit it to their sons.

There must have been so many sad hours, drifting into days that must have seemed helpless. London must have been lonely for you. The city where the fresh start bled out into a nightmare. So many things you couldn't control or understand. I'll admit there were things I couldn't always comprehend either. About you and about the events that played out, the losses and their consequences. Regrets. What did your life look like after you left and did your memories ever weigh you down, squatting on the shoulders of your every move? Or did you just shake them off as readily as if none of it had ever really happened at all? When you came back to La Línea, did it feel like coming home? And did you ever miss her or me? I accept that I am asking a lot from you, but it doesn't feel like too much. You decided your life was your own, without the space for your responsibilities. Without the room for me. It's alright, I didn't grow into someone with too much capacity for resentment. It doesn't interest me like you do, in all of your weakness and powers of contradiction. If you are still here, then how much have you forgotten and how much stays vivid, no matter how hard you try? If you have gone then I hope there wasn't too much pain, that you slipped off as lightly as you could, your last breaths observed by those that knew you as you wanted to be known. And if you'd like to know something of my life, then I'll tell you. I'm back now in the London suburbs where it all began for the three of us – me, you and Mum together. The city has changed. It isn't the place you knew anymore, but it is home for me and will be for as long as I have that choice. Sometimes, when the sun cleaves through the trees and the sirens smirk in the distance in Forest Hill, it can feel like you're both so near, two spirits at my back, guiding me towards I don't always know what. There is always going to be so much left unknown. When you first picked me up that summer morning in Lewisham Hospital, there's no way you'd have ever thought you'd one day be a missing person to your son. Please believe me when I tell you it's alright, not many of the missing ever do.

There's one more thing before I let you rest and before I turn back for home. It's about you and Mum, long before my arrival. About the times when life lay spread out before you both and every action felt pregnant with fresh possibility and the dreams you must have shared in your happiness. When the whole world was opened up to you in your youth and love. There are still times when I like to imagine you both in La Línea, looking out across the water, tiny and hopeful against the limitless blue. You might have both thought to stay just a little while longer if you had any idea just how quickly those visions of your future would fade into the past.

NOTES

1. Loughborough University, January 2020, 'One in four children growing up in homes with "very low income"' (https://www.lboro.ac.uk/news-events/news/2020/january/quarter-of-children-grow-up-in-low-income-homes/)
2. BBC News, October 2018, 'Number of London missing people cases "unsustainable"' (https://www.bbc.co.uk/news/uk-england-london-45810539)
3. BBC News, July 2019, 'Have police numbers dropped?' (figures taken from https://www.gov.uk/government/statistics/police-workforce-england-and-wales-31-march-2018)
4. Shelter, November 2018, '320,000 people in Britain are now homeless, as numbers keep rising' (https://england.shelter.org.uk/media/press_release/320,000_people_in_britain_are_now_homeless,_as_numbers_keep_rising)
5. Crisis, May 2019, The Homelessness Monitor: England 2019 (https://www.crisis.org.uk/media/240419/the_homelessness_monitor_england_2019.pdf)
6. *Guardian*, April 2017, 'London councils trying to force homeless families out of capital' (https://www.theguardian.com/society/2017/apr/14/london-councils-trying-to-force-homeless-families-outside-the-capital)

7. *Guardian*, February 2019, 'Manchester has highest number of deaths of homelessness people' (https://www.theguardian.com/society/2019/feb/25/manchester-records-highest-number-of-rough-sleepers-deaths#:~:text=Official%20rough%20sleeping%20counts%20in,city%20centre%20doorways%20and%20underpasses)

8. *Wigan Today*, September 2020, 'Police stress missing people are priority after shocking regional figures revealed' (https://www.wigantoday.net/news/people/police-stress-missing-people-are-priority-after-shocking-regional-figures-revealed-2968530)

9. *Big Issue*, June 2020, 'Government reveals that 14,600 people have been housed during the Covid-19 crisis (https://www.bigissue.com/latest/government-reveals-that-14600-people-have-been-housed-during-covid-19-crisis/)

10. Inside Housing, August 2020, 'Homelessness outreach teams reported rise in rough sleeping numbers during lockdown, new study finds' (https://www.insidehousing.co.uk/news/homelessness-outreach-teams-reported-rise-in-rough-sleeping-numbers-during-lockdown-new-study-finds-67580)

11. *Big Issue*, August 2020, 'Rough sleeping increased in London during the Covid-19 lockdown, says Chain' (https://www.bigissue.com/latest/rough-sleeping-in-london-increased-during-the-covid-19-lockdown-says-chain/)

12. Dundee City Council, 2019, Poverty Profile (https://www.dundeecity.gov.uk/sites/default/files/publications/poverty_profile_2019_fairness_0.pdf)

13. *The Courier*, July 2018, 'Dundee takes over from Glasgow as drug death capital of Europe' (https://www.thecourier.co.uk/fp/news/politics/scottish-politics/681721/dundee-takes-over-from-glasgow-as-drugs-death-capital-of-europe/)

14. *Guardian*, August 2019, 'Dundee drug death report calls for radical change to services' (https://www.theguardian.com/uk-news/2019/aug/16/dundee-drug-deaths-report-calls-for-radical-change-to-services)

15. Global Slavery Index, July 2018, 'More than 136,000 people are living with modern slavery in the United Kingdom' (https://www.globalslaveryindex.org/news/more-than-136000-people-are-living-in-modern-slavery-in-the-united-kingdom/)

16. Global Citizen, October 2020, 'The UK has denied thousands of child trafficking survivors the right to remain' (https://www.globalcitizen.org/en/content/modern-slavery-uk-child-trafficking-leave-remain/)

17. All figures relating to missing children and related missing incidents taken from Missing People, Key Statistics and Figures (https://www.missingpeople.org.uk/for-professionals/information-and-policy/information-and-research/key-information)

18. *Guardian*, January 2020, 'Councils under huge pressure as number of children in care soar (https://www.theguardian.com/society/2020/jan/09/councils-under-huge-pressure-as-number-of-children-in-care-soars-england)

19. BBC News, September 2019, '"Care crisis" – sent away children are "easy victims"' (https://www.bbc.co.uk/news/uk-49715048)

20. Ann Coffey/APPG, September 2019, 'No Place at Home: Risks facing children and young people who go missing from out of area placements' (http://anncoffeymp.com/wp-content/uploads/2017/09/NoPlaceAtHome-final16Sep.pdf)

21. Children & Young People Now, January 2020, 'Ofsted warns over lack of children's home provision' (https://www.cypnow.co.uk/news/article/ofsted-warns-over-lack-of-children-s-home-provision)

22. National Crime Agency, 2018, 'County Lines Drug Supply, Vulnerability and Harm 2018' (https://www. nationalcrimeagency.gov.uk/who-we-are/publications/257-county-lines-drug-supply-vulnerability-and-harm-2018/file)

23. Hester Parr in The Conversation, June 2017, 'We do nothing for the missing people who come home – here's what should change' (https://theconversation.com/we-do-nothing-for-missing-people-who-come-home-heres-what-should-change-795940)

24. Lambeth Council, 'Guide to Public Health Funerals in Lambeth' (https://beta.lambeth.gov.uk/births-deaths-ceremonies-and-citizenship/deaths-and-funerals-sub-site/public-health-funerals/public)

25. Dignity with Distinction, 'Funeral Costs in the UK' (https://www.dignityfunerals.co.uk/arranging-a-funeral/funeral-costs/cost-of-burial-funeral/#:~:text=The%20average%20cost%20of%20a%20funeral%20in%20the%20UK%20is,a%20cremation%20is%20£3%2C986)

26. Finder, August 2020, 'Savings statistics – average savings in the UK 2020' (https://www.finder.com/uk/saving-statistics)

27. iNews, January 2019, 'The cost of dying now meets £5,000: how to meet spiraling funeral costs' (https://inews.co.uk/inews-lifestyle/money/average-funeral-5000-meet-rising-costs-25003)

28. University of Portsmouth, 2017, 'Men missing on a night out: Exploring the geography of fatal disappearances to inform search strategies' (file:///Users/admin/Downloads/MONO%20Report%20101217%20(3).pdf)

ACKNOWLEDGEMENTS

It's no exaggeration to say that without Richard Pike, my wonderful literary agent, writing this book would never have been possible. Thank you for all of the encouragement, support and late afternoon coffees it took to thrash out my awkward ideas into the form they finally took. You are a writer's dream and I will always be grateful for your faith in my work.

I'd like to thank my editor, Jack Fogg, and all of the wonderful team at Mudlark for your unwavering guidance and enthusiasm, right from day one. I'll never forget the excitement of that initial meeting and how right it felt then, as a home for this book. Those first impressions were proven right, a thousand times over.

Friendship is what makes life worth living and I am blessed to know so many incredibly special people who make my days so colourful and full of fun. Had we world enough and time, I'd provide a comprehensive list of the people who have put up with my patter over the years. Alas, that would run to the length of *War and Peace*, so I provide an abridged version for consideration.

To Stan Cross, Megan Nolan, Charles Olafare, Josh Baines, Thea Everett and Heather McIntosh. London has never seen a finer gallery of rogues and legends. Your companionship is a daily joy and I look forward to many more years of hilarity and hijinks. It is a blessing to be connected to such special people. Thank you, for all of it.

I couldn't go much further without mentioning Michael and Paraic Morrissey, for being such good friends for so many years. I love every minute we get to spend together and can't wait to see all of the brilliant things you accomplish. To their mother, Fiona Flynn, a true one-off – thank you for all of your kindness to me.

There's a reason I think of Glasgow as something of a second home: it's a city stuffed to bursting with legends. There isn't a life I can imagine without Hayden Traynor in it. Since those first absurd days at Dundee Uni, no one makes me laugh more. To many more decades of friendship old boy. I've known Harry Weskin for almost my entire life, right back to the days when Christobal was still around. You'd be hard pressed to find a kinder man. Just the thought of a few lagers with him and Fran Gordon is enough to bring a smile to my face. The same is true for Lewis Den Hertog, Sonia Hufton, Matthew Hinton, Connell King, Siobhan Ma and so many others. I love you all.

To Lolly Adefope, my beautiful partner. I could gush about you here for thousands of words but will spare us both the embarrassment. I hope you know how much joy you give to me and so many others, every single day. There's no universe in which this book would have been possible without you. Thank you for everything.

Most of all, I would like to thank my family. So much of life is luck, good and bad. I'm not sure what I did to deserve winning the cosmic lottery and ending up with such a wonderful bunch. To my cousins Mary and Georgie Ward. And of course to Di, Cally, Danny, Mike and Holly, as well as her partner, the inimitable Luke Partridge. I'm not sure what to say, other than that I am eternally grateful for your support, love and encouragement over the years. There is little more to write, other than that you mean the world to me.

MISSING PEOPLE

We are the only UK charity lifeline for anyone affected by someone going missing. Whether you are away from home yourself, or you are worrying about someone you think is missing, our guidance pages at www.missingpeople.org.uk can help you. If you want to talk to our trained helpline team, call or text 116 000 or email us at 116000@ missingpeople.org.uk. It's free and confidential.

Missing People | Registered charity in England and Wales (1020419) and in Scotland (SC047419)